T0303836

ROYAL AND CEREMONIAL LAND ROVERS

JAMES TAYLOR

AMBERLEY

First published 2023

Amberley Publishing
The Hill, Stroud,
Gloucestershire, GL5 4EP

www.amberley-books.com

ISBN 978 1 3981 1381 7 (print)
ISBN 978 1 3981 1382 4 (ebook)

British Library Cataloguing in Publication Data.
A catalogue record for this book is available from the British Library.

Typeset in 10pt on 12pt Celeste.
Typesetting by Amberley Publishing
Printed in the UK.

Contents

Introduction

The association between the British Royal family and the Land Rover marque goes right back to 1948, the year when the original Land Rover was introduced as a product of the Rover Company to give it a strong-selling export model. It was King George VI who first took an interest and asked to have one, and it was King George VI who saw its potential as a ceremonial vehicle for Royal occasions. His enthusiasm was pursued by his son-in-law, the Duke of Edinburgh, and Land Rovers proliferated on the Royal estates, doing what they were designed to do but largely out of the public eye.

Today, the Royal family is regularly seen using Range Rovers, the flagship vehicles of the company that became Land Rover Ltd and more recently Jaguar Land Rover. The manufacturer values very highly its association with the Royal family and its award of Royal warrants by the members of that family, and there can be no doubt that this association has proved a major benefit to the marketing and sales of its products.

This book is about the vehicles that the Royal family has used, both for ceremonial duties and more privately. It cannot be fully comprehensive, because many details of the Royal vehicles have quite rightly been kept secret, but it does attempt to give an overall picture of the better known vehicles and of their uses. It is in no way endorsed by either the Royal family or by Jaguar Land Rover.

The pioneering Royal use of Land Rovers as ceremonial review vehicles started its own trend, first within the British military and then later among overseas rulers. The final chapters of this book look at some of the review vehicles that have been created in the image of the originals, and show the continuing influence of those early Land Rovers today.

Many people have contributed information and pictures to this book, and they deserve my grateful thanks. Among them, I must particularly single out Roger Crathorne and Roger Conway from Land Rover, and my long-term friend and colleague, photographer Nick Dimbleby.

CHAPTER 1

A Long-Term Relationship

Soon after the Land Rover's announcement at Amsterdam in April 1948, the Royal Mews asked Rover if King George VI could inspect and drive one. Very few had been made but, according to a story written many years ago by a company employee, one was despatched to Sandringham accompanied by Peter Wilks from the Technical Service Department. The King drove it himself off-road, and said he liked it better than the Jeeps he had driven.

In summer 1948, a letter from Buckingham Palace formally requested a Land Rover for the King. Line production had only just begun, and there was a glut of orders, but somehow an extra one was shoehorned into the schedule and had been completed by the end of July. Only about sixteen production models had come off the lines before it, but this very early example was given the chassis number of 101 (R860101 in full). It had engine number 32 (860032) as further proof of its early build, and on 29 July was sent to the major Rover dealer in London, Henlys of Camden Town, en route to the Royal Mews at Buckingham Palace.

The Land Rover was given registration number JYR 437 and was pressed into service as a runabout on the royal estates. It probably spent much of its time at Balmoral but may have travelled with the Royal family when they spent time at other estates, such as Sandringham. The King seems to have liked it: he was happy enough to be photographed climbing into the passenger seat of a left-hand-drive example during a visit to the National Institute of Agricultural Engineering at Wrest Park on 16 November. The Land Rover in question was one of a pair that were then on test there, and was actually a pre-production example numbered L31.

In this early period, the specification of the production vehicles was changing quite rapidly as customer feedback suggested improvements, and it is very likely that the Land Rover was updated from time to time by Rover, in order to keep it in line with the latest specification. One story, originating from within the Rover Company, is that it was actually replaced by a new vehicle on at least one occasion.

JYR 437 was still only a few months old on 31 October 1948 when it made a notable public appearance at the parade and review of the Territorial Army in London's Hyde Park. The ceremony required the reigning monarch to pass in front of the 8,000 troops on parade and, notionally at least, to review and approve their turnout. On this occasion, the King was to be accompanied by Field-Marshal Montgomery, who would be making his last public appearance as a military officer, and a decision was made to use motorised transport (rather than, for example, horses). The choice fell on the King's Land Rover.

Above: King George VI took an early interest in the Land Rover and obtained one for his own use. This was the first known use of such a vehicle for ceremonial review purposes, at the Territorial Army review in Hyde Park in October 1948.

Below: Endorsing the product: the King was happy to be photographed getting into this pre-production Land Rover during his visit to an agricultural establishment in November 1948.

There had certainly been precedents of sorts for using a motorised vehicle when reviewing troops. Senior military officers must have done it several times during the Second World War, typically using the Jeeps that were ubiquitous in the later years of the war, although the vehicles were not specially adapted for the task: the senior officer probably stood a little uncomfortably alongside the driver and held onto the windscreen frame for support. However, this was going to be different. The King, at least, had to look dignified while standing in his Land Rover, and that was going to demand some modifications to the standard vehicle.

As a result, the Royal Mews adapted JYR 437 for the task in hand, removing the tailgate to improve access to the rear compartment and adding a rigid hoop behind the driving compartment so that the King could stand in the rear and have some support if he needed it. An unissued news film of the event still survives in the British Pathé historical collection, and shows Montgomery looking somewhat less than dignified sitting on the wheel box in the back behind the King. The occasion was carried off with appropriate aplomb, but several lessons were learned from it.

Not long afterwards, the Royal Mews began to look at ways of creating a dignified and wholly appropriate dedicated State Review vehicle. The idea of using a Land Rover for the purpose seems to have been present from the beginning. Its all-wheel-drive ability minimised the risk of an embarrassing loss of traction on slippery or muddy surfaces, and its design allowed the monarch to stand up and be seen, whereas he was almost invisible when sitting in the back seat of a large open car, which was the obvious alternative. It is quite probable that the King himself encouraged this focus on the Land Rover; he certainly seems to have taken to the vehicle for use on the royal estates, and by this time it is likely that several were in use as workhorses and as support vehicles for game shoots.

As Chapter 3 explains, progress towards a dedicated State Review Land Rover was interrupted by the death of the King in February 1952, but there was a renewed urgency when work began on a Royal tour that would introduce the new Queen to her subjects in the Commonwealth over a six-month period in 1953/4. As the logistics of this exercise became clear, it also became apparent that a small fleet of Land Rover-based ceremonial review vehicles would be needed. The pressure was then on to come up with a suitable design in time, and by the spring of 1953 the Rover Company's own designers had a proposal that was eventually approved (with minor modifications) for Royal use.

It was perhaps not at all coincidental that the British Army had begun to think about using a suitably modified Land Rover as a ceremonial vehicle at much the same time. Ad hoc unit conversions were all very well, but they probably varied in their effectiveness, and it had become clear that a properly designed dedicated review platform was needed. By the summer of 1953, REME workshops had begun to convert a small number of Land Rovers that were already in service, with the aim of distributing them among the Army's various theatres of operation so that there would always be one on hand for a military, VIP, or Royal ceremonial visit. There does not appear to have been any direct collaboration between the designers of the Royal review Land Rovers and those who drew up the military ones – but it is no surprise that the two groups came up with broadly similar solutions to the same problem.

In the years that followed, the State Review Land Rovers and military ceremonial review Land Rovers followed their own separate but related paths of development. After 1970, when the Land Rover was joined by the more sophisticated Range Rover, it was the new vehicle that was adopted for Royal use, while the military created new vehicles on both vehicle platforms. Chapters 4 and 5 of this book explain that development, and Chapter

6 looks at one of its effects, which was a demand for review platforms from rulers and military forces around the world.

Meanwhile, the association between the Land Rover marque and the British Royal family became ever stronger. To a great extent, this association was encouraged by the Queen's husband, the Duke of Edinburgh, who considered that Land Rovers were ideal for use on the large Royal estates and made sure that they were bought in appropriate quantities. Over the years, the senior royals would come to be seen regularly at outdoor events driving or being driven in Land Rovers, and the Duke of Edinburgh would have a hand in the design of special examples for use on the Royal estates. He even took a keen interest in the design of a special Land Rover that he wanted to bear his coffin after he died. Although conventional luxury cars and special State limousines remained in Royal use, in the public mind by the turn of the century it was the Range Rover that was most strongly associated with the British Royal family.

The resulting publicity has of course been immensely valuable to the Rover Company and its successors as producers of Land Rovers. It is also noteworthy that Rover cars were supplied to the Royal family in the 1960s and 1970s, and that a green 3.5-litre saloon was not only driven regularly by Her Majesty the Queen, but is also said to have been her favourite car. As suppliers to the Royal family, Rover were granted the Royal warrant, which began to appear in publicity material with the appropriate amount of discretion in the early 1950s. Half a century later, Land Rover Ltd, which by then had been separated from Rover the car maker, held no fewer than four Royal warrants. These had been awarded by Her Majesty the Queen, His Royal Highness Prince Philip the Duke of Edinburgh, His Royal Highness Prince Charles the Prince of Wales, and Her Majesty the Queen Mother.

It is interesting to understand how the relationship between Land Rover and the Royal Household works, as it is a quite special one. Quite early on, Land Rover appointed a Royal Liaison Officer, who has typically also been the senior manager responsible for government and military sales, to ensure that the vehicles provided meet requirements as closely as possible. At the other end, the Royal family has generally provided input

The archetypal 'Royal' Land Rover is the State Review vehicle designed for ceremonial use. These three Range Rovers represent the type.

Above: The basic idea of the review vehicle was enthusiastically picked up elsewhere. This was one that was constructed by the British Army and was used both for VIP visits and for military ceremonies. (Peter Galilee)

Below: Although the design of this vehicle is very different from earlier types, the principle of providing a moving platform that allows the VIP to be seen is the same. This was built for the Pope's visit to Britain in 1982. (Kevin Beadle)

through the Crown Equerry, whose job it has often been to convey approval or otherwise of suggestions from the manufacturer.

This close association between the Royal family and the Land Rover marque has inevitably led to questions about whether the vehicles are supplied free of charge. While some have inevitably been provided on loan, the vast majority have been purchased. An internal company document written in 1987 by Roger McCahey, who was then responsible for liaison between Land Rover and the Royal family, was most insistent on the fact. McCahey wrote, 'a large number of the public assume that in order to obtain the publicity of having the Royal family use one's products they are supplied free of charge. This is certainly not the truth. As far as vehicles are concerned they are supplied at a figure roughly equivalent to inter-company prices. The Palace are most meticulous at asking for invoices and payment is always prompt. The only occasion when vehicles are loaned free of charge is for short periods when an exceptionally high number of Land Rovers or Range Rovers are needed, such as at Balmoral or a special visit to a Royal Estate by a visiting dignitary.'

Unsurprisingly, the grant of a Royal warrant comes with an obligation not to make use of this patronage in a way that would demean the Royal family. Discretion, that most British of qualities, has always had to be observed. Among the elements of Royal protocol that have affected and continue to affect the Royal Land Rovers is that their manufacturer must not provide details of vehicles in current use. Nor must the media reveal the registration numbers of these vehicles – which is of course a sensible security precaution. The details of retired vehicles may be made public, and where these are available, they appear in this book. However, readers who would like to know the VIN of the current State Review Range Rover might have to wait a couple of decades until the vehicle has been retired from service.

All four Royal warrants were proudly displayed in the administrative offices at Land Rover's Solihull factory. The picture dates from 2006.

Many Land Rovers have been taken into use on the Royal estates and are rarely seen in public. This one is typical and looks almost standard, but in practice has several special features.

This long-wheelbase Range Rover belonged to the late Queen Mother. It looks quite standard apart from the side steps that made entry and exit easier.

State Review vehicles in action. Pictured in The Mall in London in May 2016, the lead vehicle carrying the Queen and the Duke of Edinburgh was the newest Range Rover-based example. Behind it, carrying Princes William and Harry and the Duchess of Cambridge, is the Range Rover that it replaced as the front-line vehicle.

CHAPTER 2

Some Special Vehicles

It has always been the State Review Land Rovers and Range Rovers that have attracted most attention from the public, but they have been simply the tip of the iceberg. The Royal family has used a very large number of Land Rover products over the years.

Many of these have been standard vehicles that have been used purely for transport within the UK. These have acquired their own interest through the association with the Royal family, but in most cases they have had no special modifications or, at the very least, only minor ones. As examples, the Range Rover in which Prince Charles is claimed to have courted Lady Diana Spencer at one stage had a horse-and-rider mascot on its bonnet, while the second-generation Range Rover supplied for the Queen Mother was specially fitted with lights around its inner door handles to aid her at a time when her sight was failing. Many of these vehicles have been supplied in dark green, or in another green from the standard palette, as dark green has for many years been favoured for royal vehicles that do not have a formal role.

The majority of Land Rover products used by members of the Royal family were to standard specification, but there were exceptions. This early 86-inch model was specially fitted with a side-opening tailgate to improve access to the rear. It was also fitted with a heater in the rear compartment.

Above and Below: Re-registered after entering private ownership, this 2017 Range Rover TDV8 model was initially delivered for the Queen's personal use.

It is also worth pointing out that they are as prone to accidents as any other vehicle. It is a matter of public record that one early 86-inch model, registered NXN 1, was damaged when a guest drove it into a ditch. He had claimed to be a competent driver, but in fact had never driven before. Much later, in January 2019, the Duke of Edinburgh was involved in a collision near the Sandringham estate while driving a Land Rover Freelander – which, of course, was painted dark green. Nevertheless, these everyday vehicles are of only limited interest and are not the main subject of this chapter, which focuses on Land Rovers prepared for the Royal family that have been in some way special. Some of them have only rarely been seen away from the Royal estates where they are normally used, and others have only been used as support vehicles by members of the Royal Household.

Station Wagons

Many of the Land Rovers used on the Royal estates have been configured as passenger-carrying vehicles for shooting parties, either at Sandringham or at Balmoral. Their purpose is to transport the members of the shooting parties – in which case the Station Wagon configuration has been the favourite – or to carry the guns, equipment and the proceeds of the shooting events.

Land Rover did offer a Station Wagon on the original 80-inch chassis between 1948 and 1951, with a seven-seater body built by the coachbuilder Tickford at Newport Pagnell. There is no evidence of any of these being taken into Royal ownership, although one 1950

The 80-inch Station Wagon was not taken into the Royal fleet, but this example preserved in Nairobi was used during a Royal visit to Kenya in 1952. (Christopher Race)

example was supposedly used in support of a Royal visit to Kenya in early 1952 – the visit on which the then Princess Elizabeth learned of the death of her father, King George VI. The vehicle, number 0620-0003, has been carefully preserved by its owners, the Cooper Motor Corporation of Nairobi.

There is no evidence, either, of Royal interest in the seven-seater Station Wagon introduced on then 86-inch chassis in 1953, but shortly after that the Land Rover engineers began work on a long-wheelbase Station Wagon with a ten-passenger capacity. This was clearly of potential interest to the Royal family, and the third prototype was demonstrated in May 1954 to the Queen at the Royal Horse Show in Windsor, a three-day event in which several members of the Royal family have traditionally competed. The demonstration went well; Rover's Managing Director S. B. Wilks formally offered the vehicle for Royal use through the Crown Equerry, Sir Dermot Kavanagh, and Station Wagon LRSW107/3 was duly handed over to the Royal Mews. According to an internal memorandum from the Rover Company, it was used during the autumn visit to Balmoral.

The Station Wagon that the Queen was shown at Windsor had been modified more than a little by the time it entered Royal service. Undated black-and-white photographs taken in the autumn of 1954 show it as prepared for delivery. They are recorded as showing a red vehicle (although it was probably Royal Claret), and they make clear that all the galvanised parts had been painted to match the body panels, as would become a feature of many Land Rovers delivered for Royal use. Preparation work was still going on: as photographed, the Station Wagon had no top section in its rear side door, presumably because the original direct-glazed design was about to be replaced with the later rubber-glazed type.

A second prototype of the 107-inch Station Wagon that saw Royal service was given some body modifications – side skirts and car-type door handles.

The 107 Station Wagon was far from the most elegant Land Rover ever made, not least because it had been largely cobbled together from existing production parts. It seems likely that somebody may have commented to this effect (quite possibly the Duke of Edinburgh, who was known for being outspoken), because when a second vehicle entered Royal service not long afterwards, it had had a cosmetic makeover. Rover added deep side skirts and a rear valance to conceal the exposed elements of the chassis, and fitted the tropical roof panel that was missing from the first incarnation of the vehicle. They made some unspecified modifications to the fuel tank and replaced the characteristic pull-up recessed Land Rover door handles by more car-like types that stood proud of the doors. In the meantime, and specifically on 10 November 1954, the Land Rover was registered as RAC 5.

It remained in the ownership of the Rover Company until 1956, when it was returned to Solihull and sold on. Whether it retained all its special modifications after sale is unclear. Its replacement was a very special vehicle indeed, and one that had a major influence on the development of future Land Rovers.

In August 1953, the Rover Company had recruited its first dedicated stylist. The shapes of earlier Rovers and Land Rovers had been drawn up by Maurice Wilks, the Chief Engineer, but he had recognised that customer expectations were changing and he wanted to ensure that Rover was in the forefront of developments. The man he recruited was David Bache, who had been with Austin at Longbridge, and he initially gave Bache the job of updating the current Rover cars and preparing designs for a new one.

Bache probably found the rather crude styling of the 107-inch Station Wagon an irritant, and may well have offered to design some improvements. He may have been involved with adding the 'skirts' to the second Royal Station Wagon, but the result can hardly have been very satisfying for him. Before the end of 1955 he had started work on a major redesign for the long-wheelbase Station Wagon, and by summer 1956 this had been turned into a very handsome running prototype.

Whether the intention was to produce a special vehicle for the Royal family is debatable. The prototype certainly was fully painted like a Royal vehicle, with no exposed galvanised sections. It was built on a prototype of the new 109-inch chassis that was intended for the Series II Land Rovers, and it had a very distinctive front end, with headlamps on the wing fronts and a mesh radiator grille that carried a Rover car badge rather than a Land Rover nameplate. Not only did it become the next new Royal Station Wagon, but its basic design was adopted for the Series II Land Rovers that were introduced in 1958 and remained unchanged in its essentials until production of the original Land Rover utilities ended in 2016.

This quite remarkable Land Rover was almost immediately registered as TGF 640 in London, which suggests that the Royal Mews did the job rather than Land Rover. It then effectively disappeared, probably to Balmoral. It was photographed at an unknown date being hoisted aboard a ship that appears to be the Royal Yacht *Britannia*, and it remained in Royal service into the early 1960s before being replaced.

Its replacement took over the TGF 640 registration, and was an outwardly standard Series IIA model on chassis number 261-00058A that was built in early April 1962. At the time, Rover were investigating six-cylinder engines for the Land Rover, and they gave this one a 3-litre type – an engine that was never used in production Land Rovers because it tended to over-tax the gearbox and half-shafts. It is unlikely that the vehicle was used hard, however, and it remained in Royal ownership for several years.

In 1965, the Queen Mother took delivery of a six-cylinder Series IIA 109-inch Station Wagon that was specially built at Rover's Seagrave Road Service Depot. This carried her

Above and Below: Though prepared for Royal use, this Station Wagon was also the styling prototype for the Series II Land Rovers. In production, the front end was changed for a more traditional Land Rover style, and the sloping upper back body was changed for an upright design.

personal registration number NLT 9 (much later used on a Range Rover LSE) and still survives; it was also delightfully given the special chassis number QM1/2.6 (Queen Mother 1, 2.6-litre engine). Among its special features were a radio to enable Her Majesty to listen to the horseracing results, and an interior wiper for the rear door window to prevent it being misted by the breath of the Royal corgis that were often carried in the back. Six-cylinder models went on sale in the USA during 1966 but other countries did not receive them until the following year, and then in less powerful form.

During 1966, the Duke of Edinburgh also took delivery of a Series IIA 109-inch Station Wagon, and this was another prototype six-cylinder type. It was given the registration number of JYV 1D, a 1966 London issue that was doubtless obtained by the Royal Mews. It appears to have been painted in a darker green than the standard Land Rover Bronze Green, and its front bumper and all the normally galvanised body sections were painted to match the panels. Like TGF 640, it was distinctive in having no tropical roof panel.

In the early 1970s, this vehicle was updated with the latest Series III front end panels, but it retained its Series IIA-pattern door hinges as evidence of its origins. JYV 1D was clearly a favourite, because it was still in Royal ownership in May 2021, when Prince William and the Duchess of Cambridge brought it out of retirement and used it for their attendance at a special drive-in performance of the film *Cruella* at Holyroodhouse. The performance was for NHS staff and was a public recognition of their vital work throughout the Covid-19 pandemic, and the Royal couple chose this vehicle in memory of the Duke of Edinburgh, who had died the previous month at the age of ninety-nine.

This early One Ten, A444 RYV, spent many years in service on the Royal estates. The body has handgrips on the sides and rear to enable the Royal ghillies to ride on the steps on the outside of the vehicle – a detail omitted from the film replica of the vehicle.

Yet perhaps the best known of the Royal Station Wagons was the 1983 One Ten, a V8-engined example that probably spent most of its life at Balmoral and Sandringham. Once again painted in a darker green than the Land Rover standard issue, and with no galvanised elements left unpainted, this was registered as A444 RYV – another London number that was probably secured by the Royal Mews. It had a number of special features, including green leather upholstery, a special bonnet mascot, and exterior grab handles that allowed the Royal ghillies to hang on to the sides while standing on the fold-down steps. In addition to the entertainment radio, it was equipped with a two-way radio so that the Queen could always be contacted when she was out on the estate.

Although this Royal Land Rover spent its life in service away from the public, it became well known when it was recreated for the 2006 film *The Queen*. Helen Mirren, who played the Queen, was seen driving the vehicle in scenes representing the Balmoral estate. The recreation of the Royal Land Rover was convincing, although the film vehicle lacked the bonnet mascot and the exterior grab handles. The real vehicle was presented to the Heritage Motor Centre in 2001, after eighteen years and 43,000 miles in service, and is sometimes on display in the British Motor Museum at Gaydon.

The details of more recent Station Wagons delivered to the Royal family are understandably not yet in the public domain, with one exception. The 1983 One Ten was directly replaced in 2001 by a similarly V8-engined Defender 110 Station Wagon, bearing the new brand name that was given to the utility Land Rovers in 1990. This example was specially fitted with an injected 4.0-litre V8 engine and an automatic gearbox, a specification otherwise only available on some special-edition models. However, within a few months the vehicle was returned to Land Rover with a request to fit a standard manual gearbox. It appears that Her Majesty was not partial to the automatic.

The Royal Shooting Brakes

The Station Wagons discussed above were of course not the only ones that were delivered to the Royal estates, and two or even three vehicles would often be used to transport shooting parties. In 1971, an additional and totally unique Royal Shooting Brake was created, supposedly to the order of the Duke of Edinburgh. It spent much of its time at Sandringham and probably remains there.

The initial request appears to have been for a larger number of seats than were available in the production long-wheelbase Station Wagons. For most countries, these were supplied with ten seats, although a somewhat cramped nominal twelve-seater was sold in Britain to avoid Purchase Tax. The twelve-seater was clearly not appropriate for shooting parties of VIPs, and at this stage there was neither a six-wheel conversion nor an ultra-long wheelbase model like the one that was developed in the mid-1980s.

The solution was to base the Royal Shooting Brake on a conversion of the Series III 109-inch model that was offered by Carmichael & Sons of Worcester. The conversion had been developed in the early 1960s and created maximum useable length on the chassis by moving the driving compartment forward and over the front axle; the engine was left in its standard position. This forward-control conversion had initially been developed as a low-height fire tender for use in the confines of factory sites, and in fire tender form it was known as the Redwing FT/6 and used many panels from the 109 Station Wagon. By the time of the Series III versions, a six-cylinder engine was standard.

Above: The Royal Shooting Brake was a very practical fourteen-seater, specially built for shooting parties on the Royal estates.

Below: This later high-capacity Station Wagon was specially built on a Land Rover One Two Seven chassis.

The Royal Shooting Brake was created by modifying the rear of the body to provide nine additional seats, so that the vehicle could carry fourteen passengers. Most of the panels used in the modification were standard Station Wagon items, and the vehicle had three doors on each side to provide comfortable access, plus of course a tail door for access to the rearmost seats. In the usual Royal fashion, it was painted dark green all over, and had no tropical roof panel. The result was no great aesthetic success, although it was certainly practical, and the Royal Shooting Brake was registered as JYF 1K.

In the late summer of 1988, this unique vehicle was supplemented by another large-capacity passenger carrier. This time, it was based on the ultra-long wheelbase Land Rover One Two Seven model, which was essentially a One Ten with a 17-inch chassis extension, and it was powered by a V8 petrol engine. F136 NWK had a Warwickshire registration number that was probably applied by the Land Rover factory, and had a Station Wagon body that had been extended to suit the extra length of the chassis.

The extension consisted of a fixed panel with a window between the two doors on each side, and provided room for an extra row of seats. The roof, as usual, did not have a tropical panel but in this case was also raised to give additional headroom in the body, and there were two Alpine lights on each side instead of the standard one. This vehicle was normally based at Balmoral and spent just under twenty years in service before being withdrawn.

Another new vehicle arrived in 2006, this time based at Sandringham. Like the last one, it was built on the ultra-long-wheelbase Land Rover chassis, which by this time was known as a Defender 130 type. Petrol engines were no longer available for the Defender range, and so this vehicle came with the turbocharged 2.5-litre diesel that was standard at the time. Its body was constructed by aftermarket specialist Foley's, of Roydon in Essex, who produced a bespoke high-roofed design with wide-opening side doors that they described as a 'gun bus'. Although delivered in 2006, this Land Rover carried a late 2004 London registration number, LK54 XHG. It spent about ten years in regular service before being withdrawn.

Support Vehicles

Shooting parties need guns, and the sporting guns would create a most uncomfortable environment if they were carried in the same vehicle as the members of the party. So some special gun carriers have been created as support vehicles for Royal shooting parties over the years.

The earliest of these carried registration number NXH 1 and was an 86-inch model. Like other Royal Land Rovers, all its visible galvanised elements were painted to match the body panels; it did not carry the standard wire grille but instead had a bare front panel, and it was fitted with a capstan winch at the front for self-recovery.

The conversion was supposedly carried out in 1956. The Land Rover was converted from a soft-top to a hard-top configuration, and a large pannier with a canvas cover was mounted on each side, so that the guns could be carried vertically and accessed easily. In addition, a large lidded box was mounted across the bonnet to carry ammunition; this was removable to allow the bonnet to be opened.

The registration number NXH 1 was retained for a second gun carrier, which took over duties at Balmoral estate in the 1980s. This time, the base vehicle was a Land Rover Ninety, the short-wheelbase model of the period, and the configuration was very much the same as before. The basic body was a hard-top or van, and the gun racks for vertical stowage were again mounted to its sides, although this time they had hard lids rather than canvas covers. Once again, the vehicle had an ammunition box mounted across its bonnet.

Above and below: Known as the Gun Bus, this one was again specially built to specifications provided by the Duke of Edinburgh. It is on a Defender 130 chassis. (Foley Specialist Vehicles)

Above and below: Built to a specification proposed by the Duke of Edinburgh, this 86-inch Land Rover carried guns and ammunition for shooting parties on the Royal estates.

Above: The number NXH 1 was later transferred to a second gun carrier, this time based on a Ninety. (Roger Conway)

Below: G614 WAC was an EV Barouche on a One Two Seven chassis, and was a Land Rover demonstrator before being taken onto the fleet at Balmoral. (Roger Conway)

A quite different support vehicle joined the fleet of estate vehicles at Balmoral in 1991 or 1992. Unusually, this was not new; G614 WAC had been registered in February 1990 and was initially a demonstrator for Land Rover Special Vehicles, the company's bespoke conversion arm.

This vehicle had a tall box body with a stepped roof. Created by EV Engineering and known as their Barouche design, this was based on a One Two Seven chassis and was intended as a day van or support vehicle for outdoor events; its roomy interior could be configured to suit the customer. G614 WAC had a 2.5-litre Diesel Turbo engine and was probably considered unrepresentative of Land Rover products after the introduction of the Defender 130 with its 200Tdi diesel engine in autumn 1990, and so it was sold on. It was also modified: the twin tail doors were replaced by a single door and the vehicle was repainted green. It remained in service until about 2015 and was then sold on again.

The Game Viewers

A little-known adjunct to the story of the 1953/4 Commonwealth Tour is that the Queen and the Duke of Edinburgh took some time off during their visit to Uganda in order to visit the country's game reserves. This visit took place at the end of April 1954, and had been planned into the schedule from the beginning. The Ugandan Government requested a suitable vehicle to convey the Royal couple through the reserves, and the one provided was built on a very early example of the then-new 107-inch long-wheelbase Land Rover.

The Ugandan Game Viewer was built on an early 107-inch chassis at the time of the Commonwealth Tour.

A similar body layout and window arrangement were used for this later Game Viewer by Pilchers of Merton, this time probably on a Series IIA chassis.

It seems probable that the Game Viewer was designed and constructed at the Rover factory in Solihull. To the front end of a truck cab model was added a high-roofed back body with large unglazed openings in the sides that provided unobstructed views out. Access was through the rear. There were two VIP seats with a pair of smaller seats behind, and the body also contained a foldaway step or platform that could be used to aid viewing. A panel in the roof could also be opened to enable photography from this raised position. Like the State Review vehicles used on the Royal tour, this had Rover car hubcaps, a chromed bumper, and cosmetic sill panels to conceal the mechanical underpinnings. According to a Rover Company internal document, this vehicle remained in Uganda after the Royal visit, where it was used for several more years to take VIPs through the game reserves. Its eventual fate is not known.

The Ugandan Game Viewer remained unique, although a second Game Viewer built for Royal use in the 1960s drew on elements of its design. This second vehicle was built on a Series II or IIA 109 chassis, and this time its construction was entrusted to the specialist coachbuilder Pilchers of Merton. The body in this case had a rather more sophisticated design but retained the arrangement of large side openings, which in this case were glazed. Once again, there was a sliding hatch in the roof and a platform on the floor, while a pair of camera tripod mounts were also attached to the roof.

It is not clear when this Game Viewer was built or where it went. However, in 1993 a director of Pilcher-Greene (the later iteration of Pilchers Ltd) remembered it as being painted green and that its interior was 'finished almost entirely in leather with special fabric inserts in areas of the seats.' A photograph reveals a similar seating arrangement to that of the Ugandan vehicle, with two VIP seats and a pair of smaller seats behind them.

The Duke of Edinburgh's Hearse

It will be apparent from the chapters of this book that the Duke of Edinburgh was largely responsible for the Royal family's strong association with the Land Rover marque. So strong was his liking for the marque that in 2003 he decided that he wanted a Land Rover as his hearse.

The Duke played a major role in the design of the vehicle, which was based on a Defender 130 with the Td5 five-cylinder diesel engine that was current in 2003. The vehicle started out as a chassis cab, and was built up with a truck cab and an open rear back to carry the coffin – the latter requested by the Duke himself. Construction was overseen by Land Rover Special Vehicles, and from time to time in the years that followed the Duke would suggest improvements to the design, making the final adjustments in 2019, the year he turned ninety-eight. Supposedly two identical vehicles were built, the second one being intended as a fallback vehicle in case the primary vehicle developed a fault on the day. As Royal vehicles not destined to be used on the roads, neither of them was ever given a registration number.

Among the changes that the Duke suggested were the addition of 'stops' on the open rear of the vehicle – rubber grips on bright metal pins designed to prevent the coffin from moving. He also asked for the vehicle to be repainted from its original Belize Green (which was the green used as standard in 2003) to the traditional Land Rover Bronze Green that was associated with military models and reinforced his own association with the military.

The Duke was also a supporter of electric power for vehicles, and he asked for the Land Rover to be fitted with a hybrid power train. By the middle of the 2000s Land Rover was experimenting with electric and hybrid power trains for future use in its vehicles, and no doubt the hearse's power train was developed as part of the engineering programme. This delivered the first hybrid power train for public sale in the Range Rover in early 2014, although Land Rover had also experimented with a batch of all-electric Defenders in 2012.

The Duke of Edinburgh passed away, aged ninety-nine, on 9 April 2021, and his ceremonial funeral took place on 17 April at Windsor Castle. As planned, his coffin was carried in the funeral procession by the Land Rover he had helped to design some eighteen years earlier.

CHAPTER 3

State Review Land Rovers

The experience of using a Land Rover at the Hyde Park review of the Territorial Army in 1948 must certainly have fed into discussions within the Royal Mews that probably began in autumn 1951. In principle, the idea of using a Land Rover instead of an open car for reviews of this sort seemed to be sound, but it was badly in need of refinement. What was wanted was some sort of specially built bodywork that would enable the King to stand safely in the rear of the vehicle.

The obvious solution was to talk to the coachbuilders who had already built Royal parade vehicles, and it appears that more than one was asked to come up with ideas. One of those approached was Hooper, traditionally the Royal Coachbuilder and holder of a Royal warrant. Many years later, Arthur Goddard, the engineer who led the Land Rover project in its early years, thought that Tickford was another. As he remembered it to John Dean (in *LRO* magazine, April 2015),

> Tickford normally built all the special bodies for the Royal cars, and I was meant to approve some drawings of their proposed modifications in relation to this Royal Review they had in mind.
>
> Their idea was really just a throne bolted into the back of an ordinary Land Rover – Her Majesty was supposed to sit on this thing and wave at the crowds. This struck me as being an outdated sort of concept, and I thought we could make a better job of it ourselves.

Meanwhile, Hooper had gone a step further and had actually built a vehicle. Three surviving pictures dated 21 May 1953 (there may be a fourth) show a rather ungainly 80-inch with a turret-like structure mounted on top of the standard body tub. The rear wheels are partly shrouded in spats, which were a coachbuilding fashion of the time, the windscreen has been removed, and the bodywork is decorated with fine coachlines. There is a rear step to assist access, and the inside of the back body is lined and contains a pair of folding seats, while a handrail runs around the top of the structure. For good measure, the standard wire grille has also been replaced by a projecting panel with what appears to be wire gauze over the apertures for the grille and headlights.

However, the King died in early February 1952 and the whole issue of a dedicated State Review vehicle seems to have lapsed for a time, not least because the Royal Household was far too busy in connection with the accession to the throne of the late King's daughter, the former Princess Elizabeth. As for the Hooper vehicle – the only one on an 80-inch Land Rover – surviving photographs make clear that it was put back to near standard condition

The Royal Coachbuilder Hooper proposed this as a State Review vehicle, but it was rejected in favour of the Rover Company's own design. It is not hard to see why!

and used as an auxiliary review vehicle for a time; the Queen herself was pictured using it on at least one occasion.

It was important for the new Queen to visit the countries of which she had become the monarch as early as possible after her coronation in June 1953. As she would later put it herself, in a radio broadcast on Christmas Day 1953, 'I want to show that the Crown is not merely an abstract symbol of our unity but a personal and living bond between you and me.' So a Royal tour of the Commonwealth was arranged to begin in November 1953 and to last until May 1954, and in the plans were multiple events where crowds were expected to gather in anticipation of seeing their new Queen.

The Royal Mews began to formulate plans for the vehicles to be used at these events. There would be the traditional Daimler and Humber limousines, and there would even be a horse-drawn landau for the Bermudan leg of the tour. But as the plans progressed, it became increasingly clear that there would be several occasions where a Land Rover along the lines of the one that had been planned for the late King would be ideal for the job. For logistical reasons, there would have to be more than one.

When the Rover Company was approached to supply the chassis required for these proposed review vehicles, plans were already well advanced for the original 80-inch model to be replaced in production during the autumn of 1953, shortly before the Royal tour was due to begin. The company did not want its bestselling product to be represented in Commonwealth countries – most of which were already strong markets – by a processional vehicle based on last year's model, and therefore suggested that they should take over the whole project so that they could base the vehicles on the planned new 86-inch chassis.

The Royal Mews agreed, and Rover gave oversight of the project to Bob Hudson, the head of the Technical Sales Department that handled conversions and adaptations of the Land Rover. One of his first jobs was to deliver the unwelcome news to the coachbuilders involved in the earlier project that their ideas would no longer be required. Arthur Goddard's recollection, in 2015, was that he and John Cullen (the chief development engineer for the Land Rover) now mocked up a design: 'We wanted it to appear as if the Queen and the Duke of Edinburgh were standing in the vehicle – as far as the crowds were concerned – while in reality, they were half-sitting on a pair of padded bars that we had devised. By extending the rear body upwards, it meant we hid everything that we didn't want to be seen by the public. We also installed a handrail, which ran just below a Perspex windscreen.'

The First State Review Land Rover

After the Palace had approved the outline specification presented to them, Bob Hudson's team built the first proper State Review vehicle in spring 1953 on an early pilot-production 86-inch chassis, number 4710-0009. The new body was built from aluminium alloy, as used for the standard bodywork, and followed the principles that Goddard and Cullen had laid out. A simple step mounted at the rear below a side-opening tail door gave easy access for the Royal couple, and was hinged to fold up against the rear cross-member when not in use. At the sides were deep sills that concealed the exhaust pipe and the fuel tank, both of which were clearly visible on a standard Land Rover. A special chromed front bumper was added, and the wheels were set off with chromed hubcaps, adapted from those then in use on Rover cars. The rear one carried the Rover Viking ship emblem at its centre, but the hub arrangement on the front axle precluded this and the emblem was left off.

Lacking further guidance, Bob Hudson's team painted the new vehicle in a colour they believed would be appropriate, which has been described as blue-grey and may well have been RAF Blue. Seats and interior were trimmed to match, of course using leather rather than the vinyl used on production Land Rovers. The vehicle was finished by late spring, and the Palace was duly informed through the Crown Equerry, Colonel Sir Dermot Kavanagh, whose duties included oversight of the Royal Mews. A reply came from the Duke of Edinburgh's secretary, Commander Michael Parker, who invited Rover to bring it to the Queen's official residence in Edinburgh, for inspection by the Royal couple.

So in mid-June, the Land Rover was transported to Holyroodhouse in Scotland for an early morning inspection, accompanied by Arthur Goddard, Bob Hudson and Ralph Nash, the head of Rover's Experimental Department. Goddard remembered that they set the car up 'on a little piece of lawn near some French windows. Suddenly, the Queen and the Duke of Edinburgh appeared in their dressing gowns, eating some pieces of toast. They walked round, had a good look at it, and were very impressed.' The Duke suggested a couple of minor improvements, and then dropped a bombshell. He thought it would be more appropriate if it were painted in Royal Claret rather than the blue-grey that Rover had chosen. Worse, he hoped it could be ready in time for the rather grandly titled Coronation Review of Ex-Service Men and Women that was due to take place in London's Hyde Park three weeks later on Sunday 5 July.

Bob Hudson knew that his Technical Sales Department could not achieve all that was required in such a short time, but he thought he knew who could. He spoke to a contact at Hooper, and the London coachbuilder (quite used to doing rush jobs like this for the Royal Household) had the Land Rover completed on time. The vehicle looked magnificent in Royal Claret with red coachlining, but all the interior trim remained in the original blue.

Above: The Rover team took their effort to Holyroodhouse to show it to the Queen and her husband. Leaning against it is Arthur Goddard, who ran the Land Rover project. (Arthur Goddard)

Below: The first vehicle was repainted in Royal Claret at the Duke of Edinburgh's request, but retained its original blue upholstery. The padded supports were at different heights – for the taller Duke on the left, and for the Queen on the right.

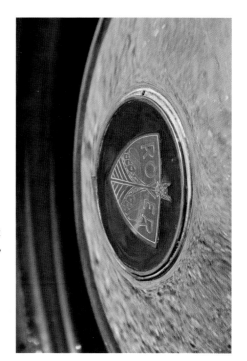

Right: The arrangement of the Land Rover's front hub meant that the front hubcaps had no centres, but the rears proudly carried the standard Rover Viking ship emblem of the time.

Below: The original State Review Land Rover remained in use for more than twenty years. Here it is in 1967 at the Royal Show in Stoneleigh, with HM The Queen Mother aboard.

The first vehicle still survives today, looking as magnificent as ever.

This prototype of the Royal tour vehicles made its first public appearance as scheduled before 72,000 war veterans, with the Queen and the Duke of Edinburgh aboard as planned, and with Air Marshall Lord Tedder alongside the driver in the front. The Queen wore a summer dress and a large floppy hat, and it was probably after this event that she made the comment that she could not hold on to the grab rail, her hat and her skirt all at the same time if a wind sprang up. A short British Pathé news film of the Hyde Park event still survives.

That first State Review Land Rover would remain in use by the Royal Mews for the next twenty-two years and, like all those that followed it, it was never given a registration number. On most of its engagements in that period its driver was Frank Spalton, who was also the Foreman at Rover's Seagrave Road Service Depot in London. When the vehicle was finally withdrawn in 1975 and replaced by the first State Review Range Rover, it was handed over to the Mews Museum at Hampton Court Palace – but has been borrowed back by Land Rover several times since for publicity purposes.

The Royal Tour Vehicles

The team planning the 1953/4 Royal tour had recognised early on that it would be impractical to take a single review Land Rover with the royal party on the full length of the tour. They therefore asked the Rover Company for a fleet of identical Land Rovers that could be stationed at locations along the tour itinerary in advance.

Again, for logistical reasons, the decision was made to supplement the fleet of specially built review Land Rovers with a number of locally adapted ones that would be provided by British military units stationed overseas. These, and others like them, are discussed in Chapter 5. The final order was for seven new review vehicles, all to be built to the same specification as the first one. Six would be shipped to Australia, where arrangements were made for some of the larger Rover dealerships to host them, and one would be shipped to New Zealand. The six shipped to Australia would be used for royal appearances in Australia, Jamaica, Malta, Tasmania and Uganda, and the Australian Army would provide the drivers, who were to be specially trained by Rover personnel. In fact, a special Army unit was raised for the occasion, and was called the Royal Visit Car Company.

The six vehicles for Australia had successive chassis numbers, which were 4716-0045 to 4716-0050, and they were built in September and October 1953. The seventh vehicle, destined for New Zealand, had chassis number 4716-0124, but was actually completed between the second and third of the Australian vehicles, in early October 1953. The team that had built the first vehicle earlier in the year now focussed on building its seven identical cousins – and indeed they were so alike that it is impossible to identify specific examples in photographs. All of them had a special canvas cover for the back body to protect it from the elements when the vehicle was being transported; it is not clear whether the prototype review vehicle also had one of these from the beginning or not.

The first two review vehicles were completed in September and were shipped out to Grenville Motors in Sydney. The New Zealand vehicle then went to the Cable Price Corporation in Auckland, a supplier of heavy trucks and equipment that was also one of the country's authorised Land Rover distributors. The next two were shipped in October to Annand & Thompson, the principal dealer in Queensland; then one vehicle went to Faulls Ltd

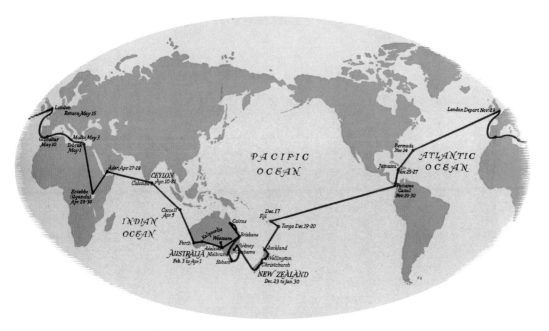

The 1953/4 Commonwealth Tour lasted six months and crossed the globe from east to west. Logistically, its most complex element was the Australian leg, and it was in Australia that most of the review Land Rovers were stationed.

in Perth and the last one to Regent Motors in Melbourne. The evidence suggests that at least four of the Australian vehicles were initially delivered to Grenville Motors, and that some were then flown to their other destinations around the country by Bristol Freighters belonging to Australian National Airways; a picture exists of one being loaded aboard an aircraft.

Rover's Technical Service representative for Australia was Ray Hancock, and he remembered the Royal tour episode as a high point in his career. He was put in charge of the review vehicles, and in a 1998 issue of *Experience* magazine he remembered working with the representatives of Humber and Daimler, whose vehicles were also part of the Royal entourage, to 'ensure a seamless passage of Royal splendour regardless of temperature or terrain.'

The vehicles were initially delivered to the Grenville Motors subsidiary of Larke, Neave & Carter, which was based in Camperdown, an inner western suburb of Sydney, and was responsible for the New South Wales CKD Land Rover assembly operation. In the April 2007 issue of *Freewheeling* magazine, the company's Grahame Jones remembered that Ray Hancock instructed the Australian host engineers to make mounting plates so that the Crown Emblem could be mounted to the front bumper bar of each vehicle. Branch Manager Leslie Moon was not amused when Hancock told him that their first effort was not good enough and they would have to try again!

For legal reasons, each vehicle was allocated its own registration number in the special Commonwealth series (with a C prefix and five digits), but these plates were not displayed during the royal engagements. It has not yet been possible to identify all these numbers, but five are known and of those two can be allocated to individual vehicles. The known numbers are C 75915, C 75920, C 75930, C75979 (4716-0046) and C75980 (4716-0049).

From the Land Rover point of view, the whole operation seems to have run remarkably smoothly. One notable memory from Ray Hancock relates to the occasion when the Royal couple reviewed 700 lifesavers at Bondi Beach (near Sydney) in 35-degree heat. The Army driver, who endured the entire event in his dress uniform, was awarded a medal afterwards!

Three of the Royal tour Land Rovers line up with their drivers on the beach in Australia.

Ray Hancock was the liaison man sent out by Rover. Here he is, adding a Royal crest to one of the Land Rovers.

Taken in Brisbane in February 1954, this picture shows one of the Royal tour Land Rovers doing ceremonial duty. These vehicles had flagstaffs on the wing; the original vehicle had one on the bonnet.

After it was all over, in December 1954 the Rover Company produced a limited-edition commemorative book with the name of *Royal Progress*, detailing its involvement in the Royal tour. Its introduction read: 'The success of the tour gave us, in this Company, a particular satisfaction for we were privileged, with other members of the British motor industry, to know that our handiwork had been of service to Her Majesty. That is why we have put together this record of something of which we are all very proud.'

As for the seven Royal tour Land Rovers, however, there was Royal protocol to be followed. The vehicles were no longer needed after the tour and could therefore be sold off, but Rover was asked to ensure that they could not be used in ways that might be detrimental to the Royal family. The simple solution was to strip them of their special features and to sell them on to private owners as standard Land Rovers; the intention was that they would then simply vanish from sight.

Although they did indeed disappear for many years, at least two have been rediscovered more recently, and it is clear that not every trace of their past had been eradicated. One was rediscovered at Cairns in Queensland in 2002, recognised by its chassis number and by the fact that it still retained a full-width seat back even though its colour had been changed to green. The special back body had been replaced by a standard Land Rover body and the vehicle had been painted in standard Land Rover green. It had also been modified over the years in typical Australian fashion, and had acquired not only a Holden engine but also some Toyota running gear.

A second one was rediscovered as an engine-less wreck in Queensland, but in this case it still carried its special review bodywork. This was the vehicle that had been used for the Tasmanian leg of the Royal tour. It had been sold to a kangaroo hunter from the Australian mainland, who had apparently found the raised rear platform ideal as a stable firing platform for his work. After a painstaking restoration, this one re-emerged in 2014, looking much as it originally had some sixty years earlier.

They Also Served

It is interesting to note that the coachbuilder Hooper also became involved with Land Rovers for the Royal tour. Records show that standard 86-inch models numbers 47160021 to 47160024 all went to the coachbuilder before being shipped to Australia. All retained their standard Bronze Green paint and appear to have become support vehicles. Exactly what Hooper did to them is not clear, but it is likely that they were given a more sophisticated appearance in some way, perhaps by overpainting the galvanised body cappings and bumpers to match the body panels.

The story of a fifth vehicle remains a mystery. It is recorded as having 'Royal Maroon' paint with Blue seats, like the review vehicles. There is no indication that 47160396 was built as an additional review vehicle, so perhaps it was another support vehicle that was simply painted to match them. When sold through the dealer Faull's in Australia, it was simply described as a Royal tour vehicle.

The 1956 VIP Review Vehicle

An additional review vehicle to the same basic design as the Royal tour models was built on a 1955-model 86-inch Land Rover, and was completed at the end of the year. This was deliberately created as a vehicle that could be used by VIPs rather than for the use of the senior members of the Royal family. Nevertheless, in later years some of the junior Royals appear to have used it, and by 1991 it was known within Land Rover as State III.

This one was most obviously distinguished by its blue paintwork, but it also had a number of other differences from the Royal tour vehicles. It was built on chassis number 5710-2615, which left the assembly line in January 1955, and the bodywork was again constructed by Rover.

The differences were mainly intended to make the vehicle appear less prestigious than the Royal ones. They began with an absence of the deep sill skirts and with a spare wheel carried on the bonnet. The body cappings retained their standard galvanised finish instead of being painted over and the hood cleats were left in place along the sides of the back body. Inside, there were two fixed seats mounted at an angle but the padded standing supports in the other vehicles were omitted. The handrail was also mounted lower down. In later years, however, body sills were added, the galvanised cappings were painted over, the hood cleats and spare wheel were removed, and a coachline was added in lighter blue.

The first VIP to use it was Prime Minister Harold Macmillan, in 1956, and many years later, in 1984, it was used for a victory parade by ice skating pair Jayne Torvill and Christopher Dean in their home town of Nottingham after they had become world

The last vehicle built to the original design in 1954 was painted blue and was generally used by more junior members of the Royal family or sometimes by other VIPs.

champions. The vehicle remained in use until the end of the 1980s, when it was withdrawn from service and handed over to the Heritage Collection. In 2003, it was put up for auction and was sold on to a private owner.

The Australian 88s

It does rather look as if Rover's Australian branch came to regret disposing of those six review Land Rovers that had been used on the 1953/4 Royal tour. In October 1956, the Duke of Edinburgh came to open the Olympic Games in Melbourne and visited Darwin, and there, during a ceremonial parade, he stood in a green vehicle that had a specially improvised built-up back body.

This may have been a step in the realisation that some more permanent vehicles were needed. The Duke's visit would certainly not be the last time a member of the Royal family would visit Australia, and the sheer size of the country once again made clear that it would be more sensible to have vehicles stationed at strategic points throughout the country than to transport one with the Royal visitors.

So by agreement with the parent company in Britain, a further six review Land Rovers were built in late 1957 in Australia. By this time, the situation had changed considerably. In Australia, the regional CKD assembly plants had been replaced by a single assembly

After the disposal of the Royal tour vehicles, a need was identified for another batch. These were built on 88-inch chassis in Australia, and were pictured here lined up at the Enfield assembly plant in Sydney.

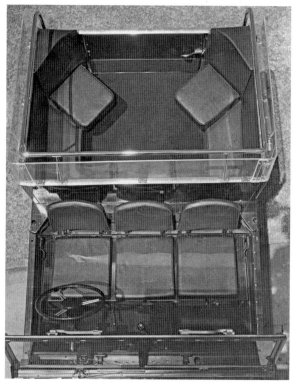

Above: The Australian-built 88s had the same body design as the British-built originals, but did not have the deep side skirts.

Left: This overhead view of one of the Australian review vehicles shows the overall layout...

...and in this view it is clear that the back bodies did not have the padded supports of the Royal tour vehicles.

operation run by the Pressed Metal Corporation at Enfield, a suburb of Sydney. In Land Rover showrooms, the 86-inch models had been replaced in mid-1956 by the 88-inch types.

Transferring the earlier review body design to the longer-wheelbase chassis was not a difficult task because the extra inches had been inserted forward of the bulkhead. There is no clear record of what happened, but it seems very likely that copies of the original design drawings were sent to Australia and that PMC constructed the new vehicles on the basis of these. The Australians nevertheless modified the design to some extent, and most of their modifications were probably made to simplify manufacture.

They used a less complicated tail door design and a two-stage rear step instead of the single-step design on the 86-inch models. As Solihull had done on the 1956 State Review 86-inch, they omitted the deep sill panels and left the rope cleats in place on the lower sides of the back body. However, all the galvanised body cappings were painted in Royal Claret to match the bodywork. The upholstery and trim were once again blue, but there were three separate seats in the driving compartment instead of the single seat of the British-built vehicles, and the padded standing supports were omitted from the rear, as they had been on the 1956 British-built blue vehicle.

All six review vehicles were built on standard right-hand-drive petrol-engined export chassis that had been sent out to Australia as CKD packs. The first vehicle, on chassis 1138-00031, was built a little before the other five and probably served as a prototype. The other five were on chassis numbers 1138-00055 to 1138-0059. All six vehicles had standard PMC build numbers as well, and these were displayed in the usual position just above

Preserved in the National Museum of Australia since 1984, this example of the locally-built review vehicles was used to transport the Queen and other Royal and vice-regal figures in Queensland during the 1960s and 1970s.

Two of the Australian-built review vehicles were transferred to the Army and are now in the Army Museum at Bandiana. This one had been given new interior trim in red.

the chassis number plate on the inside of the bulkhead. That of 1318-0031 has not been identified, but the PMC build numbers of the others were 88 1909 to 88 1913.

The completed vehicles were given Commonwealth registrations in the same C-prefix series as their predecessors, but did not always display these when on ceremonial duties. Their original numbers are not known. In the early 1960s, the C series numbers were replaced by numbers in a new series beginning with Z, and the review vehicles were re-registered. Three numbers have so far been identified: ZSF-182 belonged to 1138-00057, but it is not clear which vehicles carried ZSM-248 and ZSM-911.

These vehicles first saw use in February and March 1958 by the Queen Mother, who was visiting Australia in connection with the British Empire Service League Conference in Canberra. They were subsequently used on several Royal visits to Australia between then and 1970, their last duty probably being on the Cook bicentenary Royal tour in April and May 1970, when they were used in pairs to transport the Queen, the Duke of Edinburgh, Prince Charles and Princess Anne.

Thereafter, they had various fates. Two of them were transferred to the Australian Army for use as saluting vehicles, and both were repainted in standard Army green. Chassis 1138-00031 gained Army registration number 174-696 and a new set of red interior trim, while 1138-00059 became 174-697 and retained its original blue trim. Both were eventually handed over to the Army Museum at Bandiana in the state of Victoria after withdrawal from service in November 1982 (1138-00059) and June 1987 (1138-00031) respectively.

Chassis number 1138-00057 was meanwhile passed to the National Museum of Australia in 1984, and remains there. Two more (1138-00056 and 1138-00058) were sold to a collector and were kept in original condition until eventually being auctioned off in 2006 by Shannons in Melbourne. At that stage, they had covered a total distance of about 3,500 miles each. That leaves one of the six whose fate remains unknown.

The 1958 Series II

In April 1958, the Rover Company announced its new Series II variants of the Land Rover, with considerably neater and more resolved styling than the earlier models. When placed alongside what was now retrospectively described as a Series I model, they looked much more modern, and it must have been immediately clear that a new State Review model would now be required in order to display the Land Rover at its best during Royal engagements.

Stylist Tony Poole had been closely involved with the body design of the Series II models, and he was chosen to manage the design of the new State Review vehicle. He remembered that 'straight after the Series II had made it, I was into the Series II State Vehicle, which was my first Royal Commission! And because that was a one-off, and only me, I could take my time, there was no deadline.'

The old and the new. On the left is the 1958 Series II State Review Land Rover, and standing next to it is the 1953 model. The design of the newer one was fundamentally the same as that of the original.

Above: On the Series II model, a more satisfactory solution to the mismatch of hubcaps was found.

Below: The supports for the standing occupants were concealed in the Series II, and could be folded out from the side trim when needed.

By the late 1950s, flashing turn indicators were becoming common, and the Series II added them to its special blue identification lights.

The Series II is seen here in use at a Royal visit to an RAF base. The missiles are Bristol Bloodhound types, which served as air defence weapons into the 1990s.

As an early priority Poole called for some prints of the factory photographs recording the earlier State Review vehicles. Design work probably started in May or June 1958 with a sketch of the basic vehicle without its special back body but with the characteristic Royal feature of chromed hubcaps. A photograph of this sketch in the Rover Company archive described it as 'QLR', which doubtless stood for 'Queen's Land Rover'. This sketch also showed two key features of the eventual vehicle, one being the new 'de luxe' bonnet with its rolled leading edge and also a new radiator grille with a quite sophisticated design.

The latest developments in Rover car styling played into Tony Poole's hands here, as new hubcaps with a recessed centre had been designed for the 3-litre saloon car that was to be introduced in autumn 1958. With their central badges omitted, these could be fitted to both front and rear wheels, so doing away with the disparity between front and rear hubcaps that had been an odd feature on the earlier State Review Land Rovers. Poole also chose to use a chromed front bumper without a hole for the starting-handle (a hole was standard on the production item), which further tidied up the front end.

The rest of the body followed the lines established for the earlier review vehicles, although there were some differences in the rear body's handrail and in the extra padded

49

rolls around the standing area. The vehicle was once again finished in Royal Claret with a red coachline, and the new grille – chromed on an aluminum casting – made a striking contrast with it. This time, all the upholstery and trim was in black.

The chassis earmarked for the new State Review vehicle was an early 1959 model 88-inch, number 1419-0020, which came off the assembly line in September 1958. Its special bodywork was once again built at Solihull, but most notably had steel panels rather than the Birmabright alloy used for all the earlier review Land Rovers. The extra weight was not considered a problem for a vehicle that was always going to be driven at low speeds, and the risk of corrosion must also have been considered minimal. Most importantly, the steel panels gave a ripple-free surface that aluminium alloy could not guarantee and could also be lead-loaded to smooth out the contours and conceal the rivets visible on the earlier review bodies. A side benefit of the extra body weight, according to Roger McCahey, former Manager of Solihull's Government and Military Operations department, was that it gave the vehicle a smoother ride.

The Series II State Review vehicle entered service in April 1959 and was first used at the Three Counties Show in Malvern. It superseded the 1953 86-inch as State I, the front-line review vehicle, and the others moved down the pecking order accordingly. The 1953 vehicle became State II and the blue 1956 vehicle became State III. After the first Range Rover arrived in 1975 to take over as State I, these three vehicles became State II, State III and State IV respectively.

As first built, the front wings of the Series II each carried a standard-sized sidelight, with a blue lens for police identification. However, during the vehicle's long service it was fitted with flashing turn indicators front and rear as well. It remained in use until the 1990s, when it was withdrawn and passed to the Heritage Collection at Gaydon. Like the 1953 vehicle, it has been borrowed by Land Rover for various special occasions since.

The State Review Grille

The new radiator grille for the Series II State Review vehicle would go on to become a success in its own right. It looks as if serious consideration was given to making it a production option, and to that end a number of copies were made at Solihull. Not all were made in the same way, which rather suggests that there was some difficulty with establishing a manufacturable production design.

However, by about 1963, whatever ideas there may have been about a production version seem to have been abandoned, and examples of the grille were drawn from the stores and fitted to Land Rovers used by Tom Barton (then Chief Engineer) and Ken Twist (then foreman of the Experimental Shop). Others followed, and the stock was gradually depleted as various Rover employees managed to persuade the stores to part with one.

In 1967, Rover's importers in Iceland were looking for ways to give the Land Rover more appeal to local buyers, and they adopted two features pioneered on the Series II State Review vehicle. One was the chromed hubcaps, with the same arrangement as on the Royal vehicle, and the other was a slightly evolved version of the grille, now cast from aluminium. These were probably available in Iceland only between 1967 and 1968, on 88-inch Series IIA models.

That was not quite the last to be heard of the special grille (sometimes known as the De Luxe type). When a distinctive grille was needed for the Series III models in 1971, Tony Poole drew up a further iteration of his original State Review design, which was this time made of ABS plastic. It remained standard until the last Series III models were built in 1985.

Also new for the Series II was a special cast aluminium grille. It later inspired the production Series III design.

The Canadian and New Zealand Vehicles

Much less well known than any of the State Review Land Rovers listed above are two that were constructed later by Rover's overseas branches for Royal visits in their respective countries. One was based on a Series II, and its construction was overseen by the Toronto headquarters of the Rover Company of North America. The second was constructed on a Series IIA in New Zealand in late 1962.

The Canadian vehicle has the distinction of being the only State Review Land Rover to the factory's own design that had left-hand-drive. It was specially prepared for the summer 1959 Royal tour of Canada that was undertaken by the Queen and Prince Philip. Central to the tour was the ceremonial opening of the Saint Lawrence Seaway, but the tour became the longest one in Canadian history, visiting every one of the provinces and a number of outlying districts never before visited by royalty.

The primary vehicles on this tour were three cars from American manufacturers, a Cadillac, a Chrysler, and a Lincoln, of which the first two were fitted with landau-style roofs to allow the Royal visitors to stand during parades. However, a Land Rover was considered more appropriate for at least one military parade, and the Land Rover provided carried a fair copy of the factory-designed State Review body. It carried registration plate 71704 X when on Royal duty and wore fashionable whitewall tyres, but no information has come to light about its subsequent disposal.

The New Zealand vehicle was used on twelve occasions by the Queen and the Duke of Edinburgh during a February 1963 tour of the country. The builder was New Zealand Motor

Bodies Ltd in Hutt, a respected and long-established manufacturer of motor bodies, and was broadly similar in design to those made by Land Rover in Britain. Like the Canadian Review vehicle, it has since disappeared without trace.

Little known is the Series IIA Review Vehicle that was built in New Zealand for a 1963 Royal tour of the country.

CHAPTER 4

The State Review Range Rovers

With hindsight, it seems quite astonishing that the Series II State Review Land Rover was seventeen years old before the Rover Company provided the Royal Mews with a more modern replacement. There had been just five years between the first model in 1953 and the Series II model in 1958. Perhaps the main reason was that the Land Rover itself changed so little in the years that followed. There were detail changes, but nothing that made the 1958 vehicle look seriously out of date until 1969 brought a change in the appearance as the headlights were moved from the grille panel to the wings in order to meet new lighting regulations in some export territories.

From October 1971, the Land Rover would be further revised as the Series III, but in the meantime the company had introduced another new model. The Range Rover, deliberately more comfortable and more upmarket, was announced in June 1970 and took the market by storm. When Rover management began thinking about creating a new State Review vehicle, the choice was therefore beyond question. It would have to be based on the latest flagship product rather than on the latest version of the Land Rover. The third-generation State Review vehicle would be a Range Rover.

The idea of creating a State Review Range Rover came from Rover's Managing Director A. B. Smith during 1971, and was passed on to the Crown Equerry by Colonel Peter Pender-Cudlip, Rover's Military Sales Manager who was also responsible for liaison with the Royal Household. Back came a request in January 1972 to submit some sketch proposals for the Queen to look at. It was Tony Poole in the Styling Department who had overseen the creation of the last State Review vehicle – and he was given the job of overseeing this new one, too. As there was no good reason to alter the proven design principles of the State Review Land Rovers, Poole simply adapted them to suit the Range Rover.

There was rather more to this job than simply creating a new body, however. A 1978 memorandum written by Tony Poole explained that 'final build was carried out in the Jig Shop at Solihull, the rear chassis member was modified to carry a folding access step and the fuel tank was repositioned. This enabled the exhaust outlet to be moved to the off-side of the vehicle and away from the rear access door.' Normally under the floor at the back, the fuel tank was relocated just behind the driver. The basic chassis, numbered 355-06365B, was allocated to the job in 1973 and was built as standard. In theory, the whole project was supposed to be confidential, even within the Rover factory, but there was no hiding the truth from the Solihull workforce. When that chassis was being assembled, it had barely progressed 6 feet down the track before somebody provided it with a broomstick to which was nailed a Union flag!

The Range Rover was of course physically larger than the Land Rovers that had become the earlier State Review vehicles. The 1953 Land Rover had a wheelbase of 86 inches and the 1958 one had a wheelbase of 88 inches. The Range Rover, however, had a wheelbase of 100 inches, and most of the extra space could be devoted to the back body where the monarch would stand. As he had for the Series II vehicle, Poole chose to have the special back body made from steel rather than from the aluminium alloy used elsewhere in standard Range Rovers. It would be less prone to ripples and would give a better finish when the special Royal Claret paint was applied; panel joins could also be smoothed over with lead loading, a practice that has since been discontinued for health reasons.

As much of the extra space as possible was allocated to the back body, as the dimensions of the standing area in the earlier Land Rovers were hardly generous – especially when it was occupied by more than one person. As a result, the bench seat for the driver (and, typically, Royal protection officer as well) was moved as far forwards as possible. The result did not please Her Majesty's designated driver, who for some years had been Frank Spalton, the foreman of the Rover Service Department at Seagrave Road in London; he found the driving position uncomfortably tight.

Fortunately, a solution was not far away. The Range Rover had a 16-inch steering wheel as standard, but a prototype 15-inch type had also been made and, at this stage, was fitted to a Range Rover owned by Land Rover engineer Roger Crathorne. Crathorne had been one of the development engineers on the Range Rover, and he now donated this steering wheel to

The first review Range Rover combined tan upholstery with the traditional Royal Claret paintwork and red fine lining.

Above: The back of the body was a very successful piece of design, with a side-hinged tailgate and a permanent exterior step.

Below: The larger back body allowed room for four seats, of which two are folded up in this view.

The standard sidelights were repurposed as blue identification lights.

the State Review project. It made all the difference to Frank Spalton's comfort. The Styling Department then added their own special touch by replacing the steering wheel's standard Range Rover centre badge with a prototype of the new 'skeletal' Rover Viking ship emblem that was planned for the big Rover SD1 hatchback that would be introduced in 1976. An additional feature to aid the driver was a pod-mounted 'marching speedometer' on the dash, which made it easier to keep the vehicle moving steadily at the same speed as marching troops when conditions required.

The rear compartment, meanwhile, had the familiar arrangement of high sides surmounted by handrails, plus a drop-down step at the rear to aid access. This time, there were four inward-facing seats rather than the two that featured on the earlier State Review vehicles, and the upholstery was in tan leather that made a most attractive contrast with the Royal Claret paintwork. Not immediately obvious was a special compartment to hold the Royal umbrellas. As originally designed, the Range Rover also had a canvas top that could be strapped across the open rear compartment to protect the interior from rain when the vehicle was not in use. Later on, this would be replaced by a pair of GRP panels, because its securing straps were found to scratch the bodywork.

Construction of this Range Rover was completed in May 1974, well ahead of the promised delivery date. It was actually handed over in March 1975, and all the older State Review vehicles in the Royal Mews promptly moved down a step in the hierarchy. Although most of them would remain in use for many more years, the 1953 86-inch model (as the oldest in the fleet) was placed in honourable retirement.

As originally delivered, the Range Rover had a canvas cover for the back body, but its securing straps were found to mark the paintwork.

The padded standing supports once again folded out from the interior trim.

Above: A very British touch: umbrellas were concealed in a compartment at the front of the body.

Right: A special steering wheel was fitted to improve the driver's comfort...

...and this special 'marching' speedometer was fitted for parade use.

An April 1975 letter from the Crown Equerry, Sir John Miller, to the Rover Company reported that the Queen and the Duke of Edinburgh 'were very interested in the new Review Range Rover and were very pleased with it.' The new Range Rover immediately became the number one choice for State occasions, with the designation of State 1, and the plan was for it to be introduced to the public in 1977, the year in which the Queen was to celebrate her Silver Jubilee of twenty-five years on the throne. This first Range Rover then remained in use right through into the 1990s. It was joined after around fifteen years by a second State Review Range Rover, which in its turn became State 1 as the earlier vehicle was relegated to second place in the Review vehicle hierarchy.

The Second Range Rover, 1990

The Range Rover changed quite radically during the 1980s. What had started out as a more comfortable passenger-carrying Land Rover with better road performance had gradually turned into a luxury vehicle with a considerable amount of convenience equipment as standard. It was still readily recognisable as the same Range Rover that had been announced in 1970, and yet it was also considerably different.

Perhaps Land Rover recognised that the 1975 State Review model was no longer representative of the current breed. Mindful of the immense value of having a Range Rover transporting the Queen at high-profile State occasions, the company (by now Land Rover Ltd) probably discreetly suggested through the usual channels that a new model might be in order now that the original was coming up for fifteen years old.

Above: The second State Review Range Rover was also based on a two-door model, this time with the 3.9-litre engine and an automatic gearbox. There were obvious differences in the design of the body sides.

Below: The 1990 Range Rover of course had the horizontally slatted grille and spoiler that were by then standard on mainstream models.

One way or another, agreement was reached that Land Rover should provide a new State Review vehicle. The basis was to be the latest model with the recently enlarged 3.9-litre petrol V8 engine, four-speed automatic gearbox, and the latest cosmetic addenda, including a front apron spoiler. As for the body, however, the basic design that had worked so well on the 1975 Range Rover was to be retained, with only minor changes. There were to be solid cantrails above the cab doors, bracing the windscreen to the back body to make the whole structure more rigid. There were also to be some changes to the top of the body sides and to the handrails mounted to them. The driving compartment was to be provided with two individual seats of the latest design instead of the bench in the earlier review vehicle, and there would be the same successful combination of tan upholstery with Royal Claret exterior paintwork.

The new Range Rover was built at Land Rover in late 1989, using a two-door model as its basis. It entered service the following year and immediately took over front-line duties as State 1, while the other review vehicles all moved down a place in the hierarchy, as was by now traditional. Among the state occasions on which this Range Rover would be used was the June 1994 commemoration of the D-Day landings at Arromanches, but its time as the front-line vehicle would be limited, because a completely new Range Rover was already being drawn up at the Land Rover works in Solihull.

The Third Range Rover, 1996

The original Range Rover remained in production for an inordinately long time, not least because of its great popularity. However, by the end of the 1980s, Land Rover had started work on a replacement model, and that was introduced in autumn 1994 alongside the last of the original Range Rovers. The new one was known internally as Project 38A, although that name has regularly been misrepresented since.

From Land Rover's point of view, it was important that the monarch should be seen publicly in an example of the latest Range Rover. So in addition to supplying a number of such vehicles for everyday use, and even though the newest State Review Range Rover was barely four years old, the company began to think in terms of constructing a new vehicle based on the 38A model. The suggestion was put through the Crown Equerry in the usual way, and was approved. Work therefore began on the new vehicle.

Inevitably, the host vehicle chosen was an example of the top model, with 4.6-litre V8 petrol engine and automatic gearbox. Its special body followed the well-proven design principles of the earlier State Review vehicles, but introduced a particularly attractive variation in the shape of a stylish slope in the raised rear body sides. The distinctive combination of Royal Claret paintwork with red fine lines and contrasting tan upholstery was employed once again to good effect.

The Fourth Range Rover, 2007

The 38A Range Rover remained in production only until the end of 2001, when the completely redesigned third-generation model took over. Nevertheless, it would be six years before Land Rover provided a new State Review vehicle based on it.

The third-generation or L322 Range Rover was constructed very differently from the two earlier types, as it had no separate chassis but was built as a monocoque (essentially a large

Above: The 1996 Range Rover had a particularly stylish back body design. It was based on a 4.6-litre V8 model.

Below: Once again, the interior was upholstered in tan leather, and there was a neat tail door arrangement.

box) with sub-frames to carry the power train elements. This in turn made the construction of the special State Review bodywork considerably more difficult: the standard bodywork was designed as a self-supporting unit, and removal or replacement of any part of it would inevitably weaken the structure.

The job of building the new vehicle was entrusted to Land Rover's own Special Vehicles division. The details of what was done have still not been released in public, but the new body that was created retained all the rigidity of the standard type despite having an open rear section. Input from the Design Studio (the new name for what was once called the Styling Department) ensured a most attractive result, and the L322 review vehicle had a back body that inherited the stylish design pioneered on its 38A predecessor. This time, a dark grey interior was considered appropriate instead of the tan used for the three earlier Range Rovers, but once again the exterior finish was in Royal Claret with red fine lining.

When the new vehicle entered service in 2007, few people noted a small detail about it. It was built from one of the original production versions of the L322, which were powered by BMW engines. By the time the State Review vehicle was made public, the BMW engines had been replaced on production models by Jaguar-derived types and the front end design had been quite extensively changed. Land Rover has never commented officially, but it appears that there had been various delays in the build programme and the vehicle would ideally have been delivered a little earlier than actually happened, and before the revised Range Rovers had entered production. Not that the general public cared in the slightest, and the L322 review vehicle still looked wholly worthy of its job after relegation to second-line State duties a little less than a decade later.

The stylish dip in the sides of the rear body was repeated for the 2006 L322 model, which was powered by a BMW V8 engine.

Above: The lower part of the rear end retained much of the standard Range Rover's design...

Below: ...and concealed a neat set of folding steps. The interior this time was upholstered in grey, with blue carpet.

The Fifth Range Rover, 2015

The design of the production Range Rover moved on relentlessly, and from 2012 the fourth-generation or L405 model went on sale. As always, keen to ensure that the monarch would be seen associated with the latest version of its flagship product, Land Rover proposed to create another new State Review vehicle. This one would be the fifth of its kind, and its construction was once again entrusted to the company's bespoke division, which by this time was known as Special Vehicle Operations.

Land Rover designed the L405 State Review Range Rover very much as a state-of-the-art vehicle. It was therefore not only based on the flagship long-wheelbase version of the model, but it also had the latest hybrid power train that combined a diesel engine with an electric motor and a storage battery that powered it. This new technology allowed the vehicle to run on electric power alone when it was being used at the low speeds typical of state occasions. No official comment has ever been passed, but there can be little doubt that this approach meshed well with the Royal family's support of environmental issues.

The body design of the L405 was also quite different from that used for earlier State Review vehicles. Once again, no official comment on the reasons has ever been made. In this case, the original four-door body structure was retained but with a large section of the roof cut away, a chrome handrail around the open section, and the interior modified so that the monarch could stand in the rear of the vehicle and be seen in the traditional way.

This fifth State Review Range Rover was first seen in public on 11 June 2015 at a military parade in Wales, and of course replaced the L322 vehicle on front-line Royal ceremonial duties.

The 2015 Range Rover had a very different design of body, retaining the four doors of the original vehicle. It also had a hybrid power train that enabled it to be driven on electric power during processions.

The L405 State Review Range Rover was pictured here on duty at a parade in the Mall in May 2016. The bulkhead that separates the driving compartment from the VIP compartment can be clearly seen, and the Duke of Edinburgh is making use of the chrome handrail as intended.

CHAPTER 5

Standing on Ceremony

The Royal example did not go unnoticed. As newsreel of the 1953/4 Commonwealth Tour spread around the world, the simple brilliance of using a suitably adapted Land Rover for ceremonial parades and reviews seems to have clicked and, as the 1950s wore on, so there were more and more instances of Land Rovers appearing on parade duties with VIPs standing in the back.

In most cases, these were not elaborately converted vehicles like the State Review models. They were ordinary Land Rovers that had been adapted for the job in hand, usually with a simple handrail to provide support for the standing VIP just as had been done for King George VI's review of the Territorial Army in 1948. They may have been bulled up with additional chrome and polish perhaps, but once their VIP duties were over, they could easily be put back to standard and carry on earning a living in the usual way.

It is no surprise that the idea of the review Land Rover caught on with the military in particular. It is part of military tradition everywhere for senior officers to review their troops in a formal parade setting. Traditionally, this had always been done with the reviewing officer mounted on horseback, but horses were becoming less and less a feature of the modern military. A Land Rover had all the right credentials: it had a low range of gears to allow slow and appropriately stately progress, it was not deterred by slippery or muddy ground, it was readily available in quantity, and it did not need elaborate conversion.

Inevitably, some military units decided to create more permanent review vehicles and added extra features to the Land Rovers they converted. As a result, a new category of 'military review' Land Rovers developed. These vehicles might be used for reviews by high-ranking officers, for parades involving other VIPs, and even by Royalty if a member of the Royal family happened also to hold an honorary senior rank within a regiment. Such vehicles were not confined to the British armed forces, and examples appeared in British protectorates and colonies as well.

Other VIPs who needed to be highly visible during ceremonial parades took note and adopted the practice. Some of the instances where this occurred are discussed in Chapter 6.

Improvisation

The early review Land Rover configuration pioneered on King George VI's vehicle in 1948 was copied several times in the early 1950s, and one of the more notable examples was the rejected Hooper State Review conversion on an 80-inch Land Rover that had been built before the one that Rover designed. Already painted in Royal Claret with a red pinstripe, the vehicle needed minimum work to be returned to more or less standard Land Rover configuration. It nevertheless retained its special and distinctive grille panel and was fitted with a simple handrail and inward-facing seats in the back body. Queen Elizabeth used it in this guise on at least one occasion for an open-air military review.

Another early improvised review Land Rover was seen during the 1953/4 Commonwealth Tour, when the Queen visited Aden. The logistics of getting one of the State Review fleet from their base in Australia to Aden were too complicated, and so the local British garrison was asked to help out. An RAF 80-inch Land Rover, 45 AA 77 from a batch supplied in 1952, was rigged out with handrails around the rear body and was pressed into service for the occasion. It was no doubt returned to standard condition later.

Some early improvisations were made for events when the use of the State Review vehicle would have appeared excessive. Among these were a 1954 open-air review of Automobile Association staff by the Duke of Edinburgh (who was then the AA's president), and a review of the Boys' Brigade by Princess Margaret. For the AA review, one of the association's own 86-inch Land Rovers was adapted for the task, while Princess Margaret reviewed the Boys' Brigade from the back of an adapted 1952 80-inch model, 08 BH 44.

In the days before the State Review vehicles were available, other vehicles were pressed into service. This Land Rover was actually the one that was prepared as a review vehicle by Hooper, now converted back to something closer to a standard model. It nevertheless remained highly distinctive.

When logistics defeated the use of the Royal tour vehicles in Aden, the local RAF garrison stepped in with their own specially converted Land Rover.

Above: As the president of the Automobile Association, it was only appropriate for the Duke of Edinburgh to review AA staff from the back of an AA Land Rover suitably modified for the occasion.

Below: Review vehicles had been based on the short-wheelbase Land Rover before this long-wheelbase example was built for Princess Margaret's visit to Tanganyika in October 1956. Probably constructed by Rover's East African agents, Cooper Motors, it followed the basic design principles of its forebears, even down to the chromed hubcaps.

Dedicated Military Vehicles

These improvised vehicles worked well enough, and there would be many more occasions when Land Rovers would be turned into temporary review vehicles. However, the British Army and the Royal Air Force soon recognised that it would be more efficient to have one or more dedicated review vehicles that could be deployed as needed, and both initiated a long series of such vehicles in the early 1950s.

Army vehicles

In the beginning, it appears that four dedicated review vehicles were built, and at least one of them was constructed by 10 Command Workshop REME at Mill Hill as early as July 1953. One was allocated to each of the four major commands – Home, BAOR (British Army of the Rhine), MELF (Middle East Land Forces), and FARELF (Far East Land Forces). 11 BC 75 was probably the home vehicle, and was certainly in the UK on 7 July 1954 when it carried Princess Margaret at a review in Hyde Park of 8,000 St John Ambulance Brigade cadets. The BAOR vehicle was probably 12 BC 05, but the allocation of the others is unknown. One of these others is said to have been written off in service.

The 'host' vehicles came from a batch of nonstandard Land Rovers that had been fitted with Rolls-Royce B-series engines for field trials before the engine was introduced in the Austin Champ. With the field trials completed, these Land Rovers were redundant, and were too different from the standard military variants to be viable for regular use. However, they were ideal for conversion to review vehicles.

The Army workshops constructed bodies that were simpler than the State Review design, with folding steps in place of a tailgate, and with a flagstaff on the bonnet. There was a canvas cover to protect the rear compartment when the vehicle was not in use. These review Land Rovers remained in use for well over twenty years, and were used by senior military commanders, civilian VIPs, and even members of the Royal family when the occasion demanded. 12 BC 05 was not withdrawn until 1981, when it was passed to the Imperial War Museum and subsequently to the Museum of Army Transport at Beverley in Yorkshire. It now belongs to the Dunsfold Collection of Land Rovers in Surrey.

When the Army decided to create some more modern saluting vehicles, their choice fell on long-wheelbase Land Rovers as the hosts. This choice was made less as a deliberate decision to use larger vehicles than out of necessity, as most deliveries of short-wheelbase Land Rovers by this stage were the special military-pattern Lightweights, which were probably considered to look too utilitarian to make a good saluting vehicle.

At least three are known: 00 FG 28, a 1968 Series IIA (251-13641D), was modified in June 1968 by 34 Central Workshop REME. 03 GT 26 and 03 GT 87 (911-84842C) were both Series III types drawn from a batch of eighty-three soft-top Cargo vehicles to CL specification, which meant they had the standard civilian specification rather than the special military specification. 03 GT 87 had a particularly rakish design of glass wind deflector for the VIP compartment. The range of users seems to have been typical, and included Royalty as well as high-ranking military officers and the Lord Mayor of London. Records for 03 GT 87 show that between 1989 and its withdrawal in 2011 it was used on thirty-eight occasions, which suggests a frequency of less than twice a year. Not surprisingly, when sold into preservation it still had a very low recorded mileage of under 2,000 miles.

Above and below: Probably tired of improvising review vehicles, the Army decided to build four dedicated examples, and based them on redundant trials Land Rovers. Later given the civilian registration seen here, this one remains substantially as it was when first converted in 1954.

Above: Another 'permanent' conversion by the Army was this Series IIA model that was given a highly appropriate military serial number. (John Craddock)

Below and opposite page: The great tradition of unit conversions continued with this one based on a left-hand-drive Series III 88 by the Army. Like several others, it was operated by the Royal Military Police. (R. Dawson)

Berlin Brigade

During the period of the Cold War, the Berlin Brigade helped to protect British interests in the western sector of Berlin, the former German capital that had fallen after the Second World War, becoming part of the Soviet-controlled German Democratic Republic. Somewhat isolated from other British entities, and even from the British military presence in West Germany, the Berlin Brigade developed its own ways of doing things, and one result of this were some interesting ceremonial Land Rovers.

It was Berlin Brigade practice to provide Military Police escorts for such things as the movement of tanks, and the escort vehicles were always smartly turned out in black with white seats. The same scheme was adopted for the ceremonial Land Rovers used in West Berlin, and among them was at least one review vehicle that was made available for Royal visits and also to senior military personnel when necessary. Built by the military workshops in West Berlin, this faithfully followed the principles established by review Land Rovers in Britain, with polished chrome embellishments such as bumpers and hubcaps. What few people realised was that the hubcaps on 30 XC 16, a Series IIA 88-inch model, were not of Rover origin like those on the British vehicles. These were both obsolete and unobtainable in West Berlin, and so the ones on the ceremonial vehicle were from a Volkswagen Beetle, with a brass cover to conceal the VW emblem in their centres.

The Berlin Brigade had its own review vehicle, finished in black with contrasting white upholstery like all of its ceremonial Land Rovers. The hubcaps actually came from a VW Beetle, as these were more readily available than the old style Rover items!

The Berlin Military Police came up trumps again in 1978, when a Royal visit was in the offing. The by then elderly Series IIA was clearly considered not sufficiently impressive for the task, but there was a reluctance to transport the State Review Range Rover into Berlin. So 14 Field Workshop REME created a new review vehicle out of a Range Rover that had been supplied to the military police in 1975. The rear side windows were replaced by fixed panels with a small glass aperture, handrails and four seats were added behind the driving compartment, and the roof was removed. A flagstaff was added to the bonnet, and for good measure the standard steel wheels were replaced by the latest design of polished alloys. In this way, 56 XB 89 became what might have been the only British review Range Rover with left-hand drive.

RAF vehicles

The RAF was not far behind the Army in creating a dedicated review vehicle, and built its first one in November 1954 from one of a batch of 86-inch Land Rovers that were delivered new that month. The chosen vehicle was 55 AA 89, on chassis number 5710-0976, which was sent straight to the workshops at 30 Maintenance Unit, and by mid-January 1955

Not to be outdone, the RAF also created a dedicated review vehicle in 1954. Here it is doing the job for which it was intended.

77

55 AA 89 can now be seen at the RAF Museum at Cosford.

had been converted into a permanent Review Platform. It was finished in standard RAF Blue-Grey livery. Fitting hubcaps to the front wheels with their projecting centres defeated the ingenuity of the RAF fitters, but the rear wheels were given hubcaps of unknown origin to smarten the vehicle's appearance, and very deep side sills were added to conceal the chassis and running gear.

The RAF doubtless found it sensible to have this vehicle available, but it did not get a lot of use. Over the next twelve years, it was issued just fourteen times on short-term loans to various RAF Commands for reviews and parades. It then spent three years in storage at RAF Cosford before passing to the RAF museum at RAF Henlow in Bedfordshire, and in 1976 was refurbished for an exhibition at RAF Museum Hendon to mark the Queen's Silver Jubilee Year in 1977. It subsequently became the property of RAF Museum Cosford, where it remains on permanent display.

Many years later, the RAF also created two Range Rover Review vehicles, with serial numbers 45 AJ 48 and 45 AJ 49. Both were probably new in 1980 or 1981, and 48 was painted blue while 49 was finished in black. They had neat but unspectacular back bodies with the familiar arrangement of handrails and standing room. 45 AJ 49 was operated by the RAF P&SS (military police) and was mostly based at Cranwell, the RAF College in Lincolnshire.

Royal Navy vehicles

The Royal Navy kept one or more Land Rovers aboard each of its capital ships for shore duties, and it is likely that these vehicles had a demountable kit of handrails and supports that could convert them into review platforms when necessary. At least three 80-inch Land

The Royal Navy followed the great tradition of improvisation by creating this review vehicle for a Royal Inspection in 1959. It was based on a Series I 86-inch Land Rover.

Rovers attached to aircraft carriers did duty as review vehicles, with the consecutive serial numbers 6182 RN to 6184 RN and 6185 RN, and 6186 RN from the same batch may well have performed the same tasks. 6182 RN was fitted with a set of rear steps when it was used by the Queen and the Duke of Edinburgh, but the steps appear not to have been used when these vehicles were used for reviews by high-ranking Naval officers.

Conversions of 86-inch models are also known, and include 38 RN 20 (in 1957) and 18 RN 65 (in 1959). These Land Rovers were probably put back to standard condition after use on ceremonial duties.

Australian Army Ceremonial Vehicles

The Australian Army was among those which followed the British lead by creating special ceremonial Land Rovers for carrying senior officers and VIPs on parades and reviews, and for military funeral duties. Small numbers of Series I, Series II, Series IIA and Series III models were modified to varying degrees in military workshops. Typically, these were short-wheelbase models and the changes were minimal. Like their British counterparts, they had a sturdy handrail between the driving compartment and the cargo area, and a short flagstaff on the bonnet. Grab handles on the tail panels were also favoured. The Australian Army also took over two of the 1957 State Review Land Rovers that were built in Australia, as Chapter 3 explains.

Research by Michael K. Cecil (for his book *Tough Truck! Australian Army Land Rovers 1949 to 2012*) determined that the Army only ever authorised one 'official' ceremonial conversion, and that perhaps no more than two vehicles were actually converted. The conversion was of a Series IIA 109 GS (General Service) model, of which most examples had been delivered during the 1960s, and the instructions for effecting it were issued in June 1983.

The back bodies of these review vehicles were given handrails at the front and sides, a set of aluminium access steps at the rear, padded seating, and red Axminster carpet for the floor and sides. When used for military funeral duties, the vehicles normally towed a 25pdr gun carriage converted to carry the coffin; steps and handrails were removed, and a pyramidal structure was added to the back body to carry and display wreaths.

Later, some Series III 109 ceremonial vehicles were created out of existing GS (General Service) vehicles. The number is disputed but there were probably fifteen of them, and all were probably late 1970s or early 1980s models. These were intended purely for funeral duties, and were given special tailgates and fabric load-area covers. The mechanical specification was quite extensively changed. The Land Rovers were fitted with six-cylinder Holden 202 engines converted to run on LPG, which drove the rear wheels only through a three-speed automatic gearbox. It appears that they were never actually issued to military units but were sold off from storage; one survives in the Army Museum at Bandiana in the State of Victoria.

Above: This was the officially approved Australian Army conversion of a long-wheelbase Series IIA Land Rover. The angular front wheelarch was standard on all Australian Army Land Rovers of the period.

Below: This Australian Army Series III ceremonial vehicle is now part of a museum collection. New as a standard military type in 1979, it was later converted for funeral duties, but was in fact never used. (Patrick Sutcliffe)

The Australian Army converted its Series III ceremonial vehicle to use a locally manufactured drive train, and deleted the standard transfer gearbox with its transmission brake. A motorcycle disc brake was added to the rear propshaft to provide a parking brake.

CHAPTER 6

Imitation is the Sincerest
Form of Flattery

With the first of the Land Rover State Review vehicles in 1953, Land Rover and the Royal family broke new ground. The idea of a dedicated parade vehicle in which the monarch or other VIP could stand while being driven was a major improvement on previous parade vehicles. Rulers had stood somewhat uncomfortably in the front of moving cars in a parade, or they had lounged majestically and more or less invisibly in the rear seat of open cars, but neither was a wholly satisfactory solution. Perhaps it was the unique relationship between the British Crown and the British people that had fostered the idea but, one way or another, it soon caught on.

The Rover Company was somewhat embarrassed to receive requests from other rulers around the world for similar vehicles. One story that may be apocryphal is quoted in an internal Rover Company document and concerns President Somoza of Nicaragua, who had seen the review Land Rovers on newsreels at private showings in the Presidential Palace and decided that he wanted one for reviewing his troops. 'A message to this effect was sent to the Land Rover dealer in Nicaragua, who in turn called the Rover Company,' the document explains.

This caused some consternation. Rover was in the business of,

> making military and commercial Land Rovers and not hand-tooling for a few review vehicles. Furthermore, advice was received from Buckingham Palace that to make and sell copies of their review Land Rover all over the world would cheapen the image of the product and the Monarch. So a decision was made not to supply any further Review Land Rovers outside the United Kingdom.
>
> The factory representative in Central America was instructed to go to Nicaragua and inform the Presidential authorities that the company could not supply his requirement. This awkward and embarrassing task was made easier by a revolutionary attempt on the life of the President.

He was shot and killed on 21 September 1956. His successor appears to have modified the request to one for an armoured Land Rover, 'and the Company were able to reply truthfully that we did not make armoured Land Rovers. They came much later.'

Nevertheless, the requests for copies of the State Review Land Rover continued to arrive, and the decision not to build any for overseas rulers was relaxed – briefly, and in a single instance. The Ethiopian Emperor, Haile Selassie, was due to celebrate his Silver Jubilee in

Above and below: The Emperor of Ethiopia, Haile Selassie, was the only foreign ruler for whom a replica of the Royal tour Land Rovers was built. The onboard public address system was a unique feature.

November 1955. He had always been a close ally of the British Crown and had spent the late 1930s living in England during a period of exile from Ethiopia. So special dispensation was granted for the construction of a review Land Rover for him, using the same design that had been drawn up for the Royal tour vehicles.

This vehicle was photographed in a completed state at Solihull in September 1955, before being shipped to Ethiopia. Though very similar indeed to the Royal tour vehicles, it was not exactly the same, and a notable difference was that the sides of the rear body had straight rather than angled edges. The doors each carried the Emperor's coat of arms and, most distinctively, the Land Rover was equipped with a public address system. A microphone on a tall stand was positioned in the back body, together with an amplifier, and there was a large loud-hailer on the front bumper. The eventual fate of this unique vehicle remains unknown.

It was of course not particularly difficult to copy the basic design of the original State Review Land Rover, and even though the Rover Company declined to produce any examples for customers other than the Royal family, some copies certainly did appear. It would probably be impossible to produce a definitive list of all those that were constructed around the world, and this chapter therefore focuses on some of the more interesting ones.

These include a convincing replica of the Series II State Review vehicle that was built as an 'inspection vehicle' for the South African Police in 1966. It was constructed by Rover South Africa at their Port Elizabeth plant, and was very probably based on a Land Rover that had been shipped from Solihull in CKD form for local assembly. It was painted in Marine Grey and was trimmed in black. Following the example of the State Review vehicles, it carried bright metal hubcaps, but in this case of unknown origin. The Land Rover was pictured in the August 1966 issue of *Rover News*, the company's internal newsletter, with two of the Rover South Africa staff who had been involved in its creation standing proudly in front of it.

In Fiji, the military became responsible for the operation of a unique review vehicle that they had created out of a Land Rover presented to them by the Australian Army. This was an Australian-assembled Series IIA 88-inch with the angular front wheelarches characteristic of that country's military Land Rovers, and onto its back body had been grafted a set of support rails and a fixed rear step.

There are other cases where review vehicles are known to have been built but their destinations are not known. One reason for this is client confidentiality: the builders of these vehicles have been happy to use them in publicity material as examples of their work, but have not been at liberty to disclose the name of the client. One such vehicle was built by Land Rover's own Special Vehicles division on a LHD One Ten chassis, and had a most attractive design that is interesting to compare with that of the State Review 86-inch built more than thirty years earlier. Though much more solid in appearance, the One Ten still embodies the basic design principles of the earlier vehicle.

Much more high profile was the Pope's use of an open vehicle for public appearances. In the late 1970s, Pope John Paul II began to use motorised transport instead of being carried in a ceremonial chair on the shoulders of papal attendants, although it would be some time before a satisfactory vehicle format was achieved. The first vehicles were not Land Rovers, but the marque soon entered the picture. An example occurred in connection with the Papal visit to Zaire in May 1980, when the host government commissioned a pair of review vehicles from the British specialist commercial coachbuilder Pilcher-Greene. These were based on LHD Series III 109 chassis and were painted a dark colour rather than the white commonly used for the Pope's processional vehicles, but they were very clearly an evolution of that original design by the Rover Company from the early 1950s.

Above: Built in 1966, this review vehicle was constructed at the Rover assembly plant in Port Elizabeth. Its end user was the South African police force.

Below: The Fijian military operated this special review vehicle, which had been converted from an Australian-built Series IIA 88 donated by the Australian Army. It was pictured in approximately 2005. (Andrew Osborn)

The Fijian review Land Rover had fixed rear steps with carpet to match that in the rear compartment. (Andrew Osborn)

Above: Land Rover's Special Vehicle Operations built this review vehicle on a One Ten chassis for an unidentified government, probably in Africa. By this time, high body sides were becoming the norm.

Below: All the familiar elements of a review vehicle were present in this Series III built by Pilcher-Greene for a Papal visit to Zaire. It carries steps at the rear to aid access, has seats as well as standing room in the body, provides a handrail for the VIP, and features polished hubcaps. (Pilcher-Greene)

The Need for Protection

It was in fact the Pope's use of open review vehicles that prompted some fresh thoughts about their design. The catalyst was an assassination attempt in May 1981, when John Paul II was standing in the back of a Fiat Campagnola 4x4 during a parade in St Peter's Square in Rome. The aim of the open vehicle format was of course to make the VIP as visible as possible to the crowds who had come to see him, but it also offered him no protection against such attempts. If the modern world was going to see more of this kind of thing, review vehicle design had to change.

The Pope's next scheduled major tour was to Britain in 1982. British Leyland was contracted to supply the vehicles for His Holiness' public appearances, and it was clear that whatever they were, they would have to be armoured to protect him. It was also clear that the point of his public appearances would be lost if he could not also be seen by the crowds. The prototype of a 'Popemobile' designed to allow the Pontiff to be seen and yet remain protected already existed, and had been built on a Mercedes-Benz G-Wagen, but at this stage it was still owned by its makers and not by the Vatican.

To provide the necessary protection for the British tour, four special vehicles were built. Two were on Leyland truck chassis, and two were based on Range Rover chassis. Both types drew on the ideas pioneered on the Mercedes-Benz, combining high sides with armoured glass to create an enclosed platform at the rear where the Pontiff could stand and be seen blessing the crowds of spectators while being driven in the customary parade fashion.

Construction of the two Range Rovers was sub-contracted to Ogle at Letchworth, who were GRP specialists, and much of their special bodywork was made of GRP to minimise weight. Nevertheless, the armoured floor and armoured glass more than compensated for any savings in that department, and the two Range Rovers eventually weighed about 3.5 tons each, requiring stiffened coil springs. Both were to be finished in white, and somewhat inevitably acquired the nickname of 'ice cream vans'.

The design of the rear compartment was something of a compromise (as well as a security nightmare for the police assigned to the Papal visit), as the vehicles were armoured up to waist level but had no protection higher up, leaving the upper part of the Pope's body exposed. Fortunately, the Papal visit passed off without serious incident, and the two Range Rovers made a good impression on those who saw them in action. They were less appreciated by their drivers, who complained that even the stiffened suspension did not prevent them from leaning uncomfortably on corners.

The two Range Rovers were registered by Land Rover as XDU 100X and XDU 111X. The former was used for most of the parades, the second vehicle remaining in reserve as a backup. After the tour, XDU 100X was presented to the Vatican; the second vehicle remained at Land Rover for a time and was then bought by the Haitian High Commission for use on the Pope's visit there in March 1983. It was subsequently sold on and has for many years been on display at the National Museum of Funeral History in Houston, Texas.

Although Pope John Paul II and his successors continued to use fully open vehicles for their pastoral visits whenever possible, the arrival of the Popemobile concept led to some far-reaching changes in the design of parade vehicles intended for VIP use (as distinct from military use). The question of protecting the VIP now came to the fore and, even though it remained important for that personage to be readily visible, it remained equally important for the lower sides of the vehicle to provide ballistic protection. In a worst-case scenario,

Above: Two Range Rover 'Popemobiles' were built for the Pontiff's first-ever pastoral visit to Britain in 1982.

Below: Flanked by Police outriders and with security staff both in and outside the vehicle, one of the Popemobiles enters Edinburgh's Prices Street for a parade on 31 May 1982. (Kim Traynor/WikiMedia Commons)

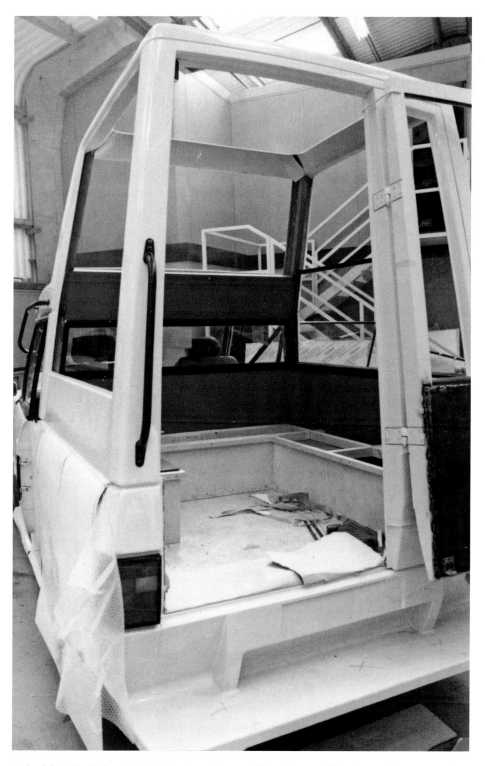

In build at the Ogle works in Letchworth, one of the Popemobiles shows the construction of its special back body. (Kevin Beadle)

the VIP could then crouch down behind the armoured bodywork. One result of this was that the sides of review and ceremonial vehicles tended to become higher than they had been – although for security reasons their manufacturers will not provide any details or even discuss the issues involved.

The level of protection was nonetheless not always very obvious. In 1982, for example, Land Rover's Spanish licensee Santana built a Popemobile on its then-current Land Rover-derived chassis, and the rear body appears to be made almost entirely of dark-tinted glass. That it must be armoured glass is neither mentioned in public nor doubted by anyone who considers the risks that the Pope runs during public appearances in some countries. Similarly, it is not immediately obvious that a Land Rover One Ten Popemobile

Built by a leading specialist in armoured vehicles, this One Ten-based Popemobile was for an undisclosed government. (Glover Webb)

built in Britain for an undisclosed foreign government in the mid-1980s is armoured. However, with the knowledge that it was built by Glover Webb of Hamble, whose speciality is armoured vehicles, it seems obvious that it must be.

The Need for Show

During the 1970s and 1980s, there was a fashion for bespoke vehicles based on Range Rovers among the very wealthy in some countries, especially in Asia and the Middle East. Several British specialist companies catered for this, and some quite spectacular creations appeared. It was inevitable that the rulers of some of these countries would request ceremonial or review vehicles in the same vein, and of course they turned to the same specialist companies to have them built. Among those companies were FLM Panelcraft in London, and Glenfrome in Bristol.

FLM Panelcraft had built a number of special Range Rover conversions for the Libyan leader Colonel Gaddafi, and they were therefore a natural choice when he wanted a vehicle from which to review his military troops some time around 1980. The one they built had a most unusual design, adapted from the convertible Range Rover body that the company already had in production. With a fixed roof above the driving compartment, and a short handrail at its rear edge, it was open at the rear and had curved side glasses behind the door pillars. The standard rear seat remained in place but with the centre of its cushion removed so that Gaddafi could stand on the seat pan. Behind the seat was a trimmed and padded pillar, against which he could lean for support.

The Gaddafi vehicle was based on a two-door Range Rover, but a four-door model was used as the basis of another remarkable conversion that Glenfrome built in 1984 for the Sultan of Brunei. The Sultan was of course known to be one of the world's richest men and also to have a huge collection of exotic cars, so it was no surprise that he should have ordered such a vehicle.

Interestingly, the two rear side doors were welded closed and panelled over, leaving only their windows visible on the finished vehicle. The front of the vehicle featured Glenfrome's four-headlamp design, and the rear of the body provided a standing platform, handrails for support, and a small windscreen for the Sultan, as well as a set of steps for access. The whole vehicle was painted, perhaps predictably, in metallic gold.

Above: The review vehicle that FLM Panelcraft built for Libya's Colonel Ghadaffi was based on the coachbuillder's convertible derivative of a two-door Range Rover. (FLM Panelcraft)

Below: The centre of the seat was removed to give Ghadaffi somewhere to stand, and he could lean against the padded pillar if he needed to. (FLM Panelcraft)

Specialist coachbuilder Glenfrome turned its hand to review vehicles with this Range Rover, built for the Sultan of Brunei in 1984. (Glenfrome)

Above and below: There are still many mysteries associated with review and ceremonial vehicles built from Land Rovers around the world. Here is one to end the book. This Series I was photographed in the late 1950s, supposedly in New Zealand. It appears to have been converted from a Station Wagon, and still bears Station Wagon badges front and rear. But who did it, and why?